Sustainability Decoded

How to Unlock Profit Through the Value Chain

Laura Musikanski

Executive Director and Co-Founder,
The Happiness Initiative
Email: **laura.musikanski@gmail.com**

First published in 2013 by Dō Sustainability
87 Lonsdale Road, Oxford OX2 7ET, UK

Copyright © 2013 Laura Musikanski

The moral right of the author has been asserted.

ISBN 978-1-909293-58-8 (eBook-ePub)
ISBN 978-1-909293-59-5 (eBook-PDF)
ISBN 978-1-909293-57-1 (Paperback)

A catalogue record for this title is available from the British Library.

Dō Sustainability strives for net positive social and environmental impact. See our sustainability policy at **www.dosustainability.com**.

Page design and typesetting by Alison Rayner
Cover by Becky Chilcott

For further information on Dō Sustainability, visit our website:
www.dosustainability.com

DōShorts

Dō Sustainability is the publisher of **DōShorts**: short, high-value ebooks that distil sustainability best practice and business insights for busy, results-driven professionals. Each DōShort can be read in 90 minutes.

New and forthcoming DōShorts – stay up to date

We publish 3 to 5 new DōShorts each month. The best way to keep up to date? Sign up to our short, monthly newsletter. Go to **www.dosustainability.com/newsletter** to sign up to the Dō Newsletter. Some of our latest and forthcoming titles include:

- *Full Product Transparency: Cutting the Fluff Out of Sustainability* Ramon Arratia

- *Making the Most of Standards* Adrian Henriques

- *How to Account for Sustainability: A Business Guide to Measuring and Managing* Laura Musikanski

- *Sustainability in the Public Sector: An Essential Briefing for Stakeholders* Sonja Powell

- *Sustainability Reporting for SMEs: Competitive Advantage Through Transparency* Elaine Cohen

- *REDD+ and Business Sustainability: A Guide to Reversing Deforestation for Forward Thinking Companies* Brian McFarland

- *How Gamification Can Help Your Business Engage in Sustainability* Paula Owen

- *Sustainable Energy Options for Business* Philip Wolfe

- *Adapting to Climate Change: 2.0 Enterprise Risk Management*
  Mark Trexler & Laura Kosloff

- *How to Engage Youth to Drive Corporate Responsbility: Roles and Interventions*   Nicolò Wojewoda

- *The Short Guide to Sustainable Investing*   Cary Krosinsky

- *Strategic Sustainability: Why it Matters to Your Business and How to Make it Happen*   Alexandra McKay

Subscriptions

In addition to individual sales of our ebooks, we now offer subscriptions. Access 60+ ebooks for the price of 5 with a personal subscription to our full e-library. Institutional subscriptions are also available for your staff or students. Visit **www.dosustainability.com/books/subscriptions** or email **veruschka@dosustainability.com**

Write for us, or suggest a DōShort

Please visit **www.dosustainability.com** for our full publishing programme. If you don't find what you need, write for us! Or suggest a DōShort on our website. We look forward to hearing from you.

Abstract

SUSTAINABILITY DECODED is a business book that provides a no-nonsense, profitable means to practice sustainability. It is the only book of its kind that starts with the value chain, the tried and true foundation of any business, and identifies where and how you can integrate sustainability into the stations along that chain. It provides innovative tools and approaches for each station, enabling the reader to hone his or her business skills and for a business to successfully practice sustainability.

It is as useful to the non-business person who needs a quick orientation to business as it is to the long time business professional who is looking for practical and profitable inspiration from sustainability.

The book provides tools at the end of each chapter which the reader can use in the business context and/or for his or her professional development. These tools include:

- Sustainability Matrix Decision Tool for Codes of Conduct

- Triple Bottom Line Short Form

- Eco-Label Graphic Matrix

- Sustainability Ratio Guide

- Life Cycle Analysis Grid

- Local-Global Scorecard

ABSTRACT

- The Redesign Card

- The Green IT Checklist

- The Balanced Scorecard for Life

- The Biomimcry Backwards Forwards Tool

About the Author

 **LAURA MUSIKANSKI**, JD, MBA, is Executive Director and Co-Founder of The Happiness Initiative (www. happycounts.org). Prior to joining the Happiness Initiative, Laura served as Executive Director of Sustainable Seattle, and before that she was the Sustainability Director for a medium-sized (US$90m a year) environmental consulting firm and an entrepreneur and small business owner for 18 years. She taught on the University of Washington MBA program as well as for professional training programs. Laura is a lawyer with an MBA and certificates in Environmental Management and Environmental Law and Regulations from the University of Washington. She is a member of the Balaton Group (www.balatongroup.org), and has published articles in *YES*, *Earth Island Institute*, *CSRWire*, *Mom's Rising*, and *The Progressive*.

Acknowledgments

THANK YOU to Clinton Bliss for his support and advice. Thank you to Ann Prezyna for her friendship and all she gives. Thank you to Arthur George for his help. Thank you to Ann Burgund for her inspiration. Thank you to Michael Roberts for his input. Thank you to Karen Jhoh for her love.

Who Can Use This Book

- C-suite executives and managers who are looking to bring cohesion to a company with multiple sustainability practices while at the same time looking to improve business performance through sustainability

- Entrepreneurs and innovators who are looking for inspiration or the foundation for innovation for sustainability and business

- Beginning business students seeking to understand the landscape of business and its fit with sustainability

- Scientists, engineers, programmers and other non-business trained professionals who can benefit from a quick orientation to business while gathering information about sustainability practices

- Students from non-business colleges working on business case problems, challenges or competitions, particularly within an interdisciplinary team or program.

Contents

CHAPTER 1

Introduction –
Do Good, Make Good

WE WILL BE SUSTAINABLE when companies make more of a profit *because* they integrate sustainability into their processes, goods and services and so contribute to the longevity of our planet and the happiness of all people. There are many books that make the business case for sustainability. This book maps out practical approaches for making a profit through sustainability.

This book is designed to help business managers save the planet while increasing profits. My theory is that the best approach to sustainability is based on tried and true practices, and so we will use the value chain – the backbone of every business. I present practical, clear and adaptable sustainability practices that can be applied to the value chain.

The value chain

Michael Porter introduced the 'value chain' in 1985.[1] He classified a sequence of basic activities that a business undertakes to create a good or service. There are primary activities and support activities. Primary activities are:

- Logistics

- Operations

- Marketing and sales

- Service

Support activities are:

- Infrastructure

- Human resources

- Technology

- Procurement.

FIGURE 1. The value chain with primary and supporting activities

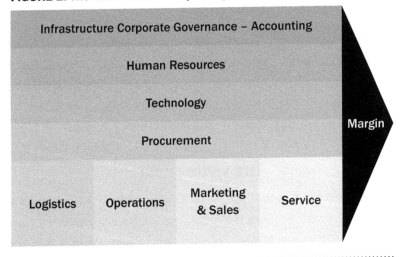

Porter's message was that each activity represents an opportunity to increase the company's competitive advantage. In this book, we will look at the activities on the value chain as entry points for taking action on sustainability, while increasing profits and your competitive advantage.

The sustainability activities we will look at are:

- Corporate responsibility

- Triple bottom line accounting

- Eco-labels

- Natural resource-based procurement

- Life cycle analysis

- Local economies

- Reduce, reuse, recycle, redesign

- Green buildings

- Work–life balance

- Biomimicry (emulating nature).

These sustainability activities are mapped to Porter's value chain so that you that can tailor sustainability to your business and take action. For clarity, I break infrastructure into corporate governance and accounting and separate technology into information technology and research and development.

FIGURE 2. Value chain activities and sustainability activities

VALUE CHAIN ACTIVITIES	SUSTAINABILITY ACTIVITIES
Corporate governance	Corporate responsibility
Accounting	Triple bottom line accounting
Marketing & sales	Eco-labels
Procurement	Natural resource-based procurement
Operations	Life cycle analysis
Logistics	Local economies
Service	Reduce, reuse, recycle, redesign
Information technology	Green buildings
Human resources	Work–life balance
Research & development	Biomimicry

How to use this book

This book is designed to be useful at any point. You can read it front to back, skip around chapters, or even read it back to front. Each chapter begins with a short description of a value chain station and explains a tried and true sustainability practice in the context of that value chain station. There are two case studies that explore how a business has integrated sustainability into every station on the value chain. In this way you get the basics of sustainability in as distilled and useful a format as possible.

Each chapter concludes with a tool for easy integration of sustainability into your business process or product. As you read this book, I encourage you to think about how the sustainability practices introduced in one section could be useful in another station on the value chain.

....

CHAPTER 2

Corporate Governance and Corporate Responsibility

Corporate governance: Keeping it real

CORPORATE GOVERNANCE can be a befuddling concept. It comes from the top: the board, CEO and other executives. But what is it? The Organization for Economic Cooperation and Development (OECD) defines it as 'the system by which business corporations are directed and controlled'. Corporate governance has three parts:

- Stakeholders

- Rules

- Procedures

Stakeholders are 'any group or individual who can affect or is affected by the achievement of the organization's objectives'.[2] Rules ensure accountability. They include roles and responsibilities, risk management systems and performance tracking. Procedures are formed after the policies such as the mission statement, vision, core values and codes of conduct.

What makes sustainability stick?

It comes from the top. No matter how robust a company's sustainability program, how passionate the staff or how ready the marketplace, for a company to be successful in its sustainability programs there must be support from the top. This means there must be a policy and that resources are allocated and performance is tracked with supervision from the top. The simplest way to demonstrate support from the top is to adopt a code of conduct.

About a code of conduct . . .

A code of conduct sets out the principles to guide decisions.[3] Codes of conduct vary in their specificity:[4]

- Procedurally, in their formalized rules dictating behavior.

- Legally, in requiring compliance and setting a bar for behavior.

- In being principle-based, orienting employees and managers toward continual improvement, leading to sustainability and profit.

They also vary in terms of area of focus:[5]

- General business performance.

- Environmental management, often focused on stewardship.

- Industry focus, e.g. the Equator Principles for the banking sector; the Electronic Industries Code of Conduct (EICC) for the information technology industry; Kimberly Principles for the diamond industry; and the apparel industry Partnership Agreement.

- Human rights protection, often aimed at suppliers, and based on the International Labor Organization's (ILO) principles.

About 85% of companies in the United States have at least one code of conduct.[6] Most companies adopt several codes of conduct for different areas of business performance rather than one overarching set of principles.[7]

Which code?

Before you craft or modify a code of conduct for your company you need to know about the nine basic codes for general business performance. These are the touchstones for any code of conduct. They are:[8]

1. OECD Guidelines for Multinational Enterprise

2. UN Global Compact

3. Principles for Global Corporate Responsibility: Benchmarks

4. Caux Principles for Business

5. Human Rights Principles and Responsibilities for TNCs and Other Business Enterprises

6. Global Sullivan Principles

7. CERES Principles

8. International Chamber of Commerce Business Charter for Sustainable Development

9. The ISO 26000 Guidelines for Social Responsibility

The three sets of principles that capture the widest diversity of interest are the OECD Guideline for Multinational Enterprises, the Global Compact and the UN's Human Rights Principles and Responsibilities for TNCs and Other Business Enterprises.[9]

The OECD Guidelines are broad in scope, including economic, social and environmental aspects, but its principles are not concise and include references to other principles such as those of the International Labor Organization. The ISO 2600 guidelines are not so much standards but instead help define social responsibility. It can be used to decide performance to be managed and areas for stakeholder engagement.

The UN Global Compact is the brainchild of the former UN Secretary-General Kofi Annan. Companies register as a participant, commit to implement the principles, file an annual report or 'communication on progress' (COP) and can use the Global Compact logo. If a company misses the deadline in filing its COP two years running, it is de-listed. This is one of the most robust organizations, offering companies opportunities to learn about corporate social responsibility (CSR) in theory and practice and collaborate with other companies and agencies.

The Principles for Global Corporate Responsibility: Benchmarks (Benchmarks) is one of the most extensive set of principles with the largest scope.[10] It is also one of the easiest to read, written in plain English. It is issued and used by the religious sector and used by The Interfaith Center on Corporate Responsibility as a basis for shareholder resolutions.

The UN's Human Rights Principles and Responsibilities for TNCs and Other Business Enterprises is fairly complex and written in 'legalese'. It is most applicable to companies operating in countries where human rights are abused.

The last three principles are less general in scope. The Global Sullivan Principles covers human rights, and both the International Chamber of Commerce Business Charter for Sustainable Development and the CERES Principles cover environmental performance.

Your sustainability code of conduct

When adopting your code of conduct, you can state that your company follows one of the sets of principles listed above or from another agency for general performance. For specific areas of performance, you will want to craft more specific codes. Your code of conduct should follow my CLEAR criteria:

FIGURE 3. CLEAR criteria for codes of conduct

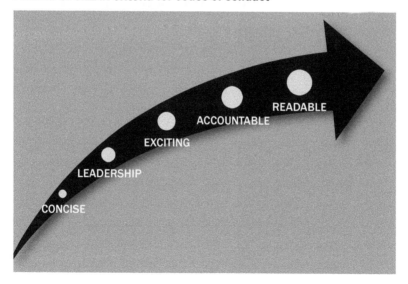

- Concise – states the meaning in a simple way that is understandable for all levels.

- Leadership – fits within the company's mission and vision and is within the sustainability context.

- Exciting – inspires innovation leading to continual improvement, to new ways of doing things, to new products and services.

- Accountable – can be measured and verified.

- Readable – aims for 10 minutes or less, no legalese nor too technical.

When it is time?
The Sustainability Matrix decision tool

At what level should your company implement a sustainability program? The BCG Matrix is a tried and true tool for determining when to keep, sell or invest in a product or service. The Sustainability Matrix, modeled after the BCG Matrix, helps you decide which approach you should take.

On one axis lies the ability of the environment, society and economy to support continued operations of a business. On the other axis lies the impact of a business on the planet. Using the matrix requires an analysis of the environmental, social and greater economic resources upon which a business product line or business entity depends. Rather than attempting to analyze every resource, you are better off identifying the one or two resources most needed to continue operations. It also requires understanding the scale of impact compared to the other businesses in the industry. From here, you can place yourself on the matrix.

FIGURE 4. The Sustainability Matrix

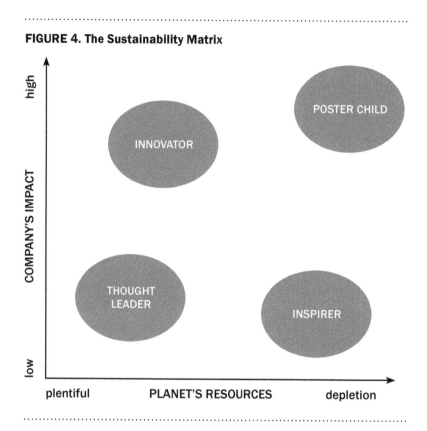

Sustainability Matrix for corporate responsibility decision approaches:

- **Poster Child:** Your company is in a high-risk/high-reward situation. Take an ethical approach to your corporate responsibility. You are likely to attract attention with your sustainability program. Before issuing a code of conduct, establish your sustainability programs, accomplishments and goals. Once you do adopt your code of conduct, clearly communicate your goals, long-term plans, and vision of your company's role in the path to sustainability. Industries with companies likely to be in this sector: oil and gas, water, automotive, mining, manufactured goods, textiles.

- **Innovator:** Your company is in a low-risk/high-reward situation. Take a managerial approach. You can adopt a code of conduct at the same time as you start your sustainability programs. Your company's success in sustainability has a higher chance if your programs are innovative, providing new products or new production processes. Your code of conduct should emphasize innovation. Industries with companies likely to be in this sector: technology, telecommunications, health care, energy (other than oil and gas), organics.

- **Inspirer:** Your company is in a high-risk/low-reward situation. Take a strategic approach. Put your company in a position where it can take a strong stance with its code of conduct and ensure there is follow-through. Otherwise you run the risk of accusations of misleading your customers. Industries likely to be in this sector: chocolate, airline, arms, chemicals, leisure, pharmaceuticals.

- **Thought Leader:** Your company is in a low-risk/low-reward situation. Take an innovative approach. Thought Leader companies are already providing solutions to sustainability challenges with the goods or services they offer. Integrating sustainability into the value chain is an easy step. To become a leader in the industry, it will be necessary to provide new solutions. Industries with companies likely to be in this sector: bicycles, hybrids, waste reduction, other 'green' industries.

CHAPTER 3

Financial Accounting and Triple Bottom Line Accounting

Financial accounting straight up

FINANCIAL ACCOUNTING TELLS THE STORY of business success and failure – in terms of profit. Every year a company issues financial statements. In the United States, companies that sell shares on the stock market or with over 500 shareholders are required by law to file with the Securities and Exchange Commission (SEC). Their reports must conform to Generally Accepted Accounting Principles (GAAP). Companies also must put their financial statements on their website. Smaller companies and privately held companies don't have to make their financial statements public, but they do need to have them to file their taxes. Essentially, all businesses issue financial statements.

Financial statements come in four parts:

- Balance sheet: all of the company's assets (everything the company owns, from money to equipment), liabilities (the company's debts) and equity (the shares)

- Income statement: all of the revenues (sales from goods and services to equipment and business units), expenses (costs to do business) and profits

- Statement of retained earnings: the profits, less the dividends paid to shareholders in that year

- Cash flow statement: the amount of cash the company started within the period, the amount of cash spent (to operate and on investments and to pay debts) and the amount of cash at the end of the period

Measure, manage, measure

The flip side of the old business adage 'you can't manage what you don't measure' is 'you get what you measure'. If short-term profit is the only measurement you use, other aspects of business performance go unmeasured and therefore unmanaged. If short- and long-term profit as well as environmental, social and wider economic performance is measured, a business is being managed for sustainability – its own and the planet's.

Triple bottom line accounting: What is it and who is doing it?

Triple bottom line reporting tells the story of business success and failure – in terms of environmental, social and economic performance and business impacts on the environment, society and economy. Triple bottom line reporting is voluntary in the United States. A few countries, including Denmark, Sweden and Australia, require some aspects of triple bottom line reporting for large businesses, businesses partly owned by the government or governmental agencies.[12]

In 1992, 27 companies issued some form of triple bottom line report.[11]

Back then, most companies reported only environmental performance. In 2012, 9000 companies issued some form of sustainability report, up from 3600 in 2010. Most now cover economic, social and environmental performance.

What do you measure?

The Global Reporting Initiative is the world's most prominent set of sustainability accounting guidelines.[13] Most triple bottom line reports follow these guidelines, or are informed by the GRI's 'areas of sustainability'.[14] That is one answer to what you measure for triple bottom line reporting.

The real answer to the question of what to measure is found in the tried and true business practice of continual improvement. Continual improvement comes in two forms:

- Small incremental steps to eliminate waste and unnecessary activities

- Large-scale or radical changes to improve processes and products

But it's not just the guidelines or metrics that matter when accounting for sustainability. Your people matter. W. Edwards Deming, known for his qualitative methods in quality improvement, understood that employees hold the key to unlocking opportunities for continual improvement.[15] He created a 'system of profound knowledge' that today is known as 'kaizen' which is guided by four principles:

- Systems thinking

- Equal emphasis on process and results

- Open-minded non-judgmental perspective between managers and their employees

- Encouragement by managers for their employees to learn and by upper management for managers to learn from their employees

Measuring – and reporting – sustainability can be an expensive and onerous task if undertaken on its own. Instead, it is better to measure environmental, social and economic performance with the goal of continual improvement for quality, profit and environmental, social and economic performance. It is also necessary to educate your managers about sustainability reporting and orient them to working with their employees to uncover opportunities for continual improvement to sustainability performance and profit. Measure the impact of actions taken, and then repeat the process.

Your company and the triple bottom line

My tool, the Triple Bottom Line Short Form, helps you to frame sustainability into opportunities for your company. This tool will do two things:

- Give you an overall understanding of what goes into a sustainability report.

- Provide you with a template for continual improvement in sustainability and profitability.

To use this tool, describe your company and your business performance. Include past activities. Put the tool down for a day, then come back to it and write down any ideas you have for continual improvement. Repeat the process with your managers, and encourage them to obtain input from their employees. From there, determine what you will measure and manage over a designated time period. It is important to link your company's profit measures with the sustainability measures you use.

....

FIGURE 5. The Triple Bottom Line Short Form

The Triple Bottom Line Short Form – About Us

Name of organization:

Short explanation of services/goods supplied:

Mission and purpose statement:

Short history of organization:

The Triple Bottom Line Report Short Form – Economic, Part 1

Financial performance – revenue, costs and profit:

Percentage of costs represented by locally based suppliers:

Total employee compensation:

Percentage of top management hired from local community:

Donations and community investments:

Description of indirect economic impacts – jobs, skill enhancement, change in productivity for business or industry:

The Triple Bottom Line Report Short Form – Economic, Part 2

Sustainability or life cycle assessments of products or services:

Marketing and communication policies and practices:

Public policy positions, participation and political contributions:

Policies, programs and practices to manage impact of operations on communities:

The Triple Bottom Line Short Form – Social, Part I

Total workforce by category (entry, management, top management):

Workforce diversity (age, gender, ethnicity) by category:

Board of directors' diversity:

Employee benefits for full-time and part-time:

Inclusion and/or anti-discrimination policy:

Activities regarding inclusion and/or anti-discrimination policy:

The Triple Bottom Line Short Form – Social, Part 2

Employee training and education programs and average hours of training per year per employee by category:

Supplier or procurement policy (protecting human rights and other sustainability-related impacts):

Activities regarding the supplier or procurement policy:

Description of policies or programs regarding indigenous peoples and/or vulnerable populations:

The Triple Bottom Line Short Form – Environmental, Part I

Greenhouse gas emissions inventory:

Methodology and assumptions for greenhouse gas inventory:

Programs to manage greenhouse gas emissions:

Energy consumption:

Policies and programs regarding energy efficiency:

Policies and programs regarding alternative energy:

The Triple Bottom Line Short Form – Environmental, Part 2

Assessment of impact on environment from transportation of goods or services:

Materials used (type and amount) to produce goods and services:

Percent of materials used that are recycled, recyclable, waste-free, FSC certified, organic or eco-friendly:

Waste produced:

Policies and practices to reduce waste:

The Triple Bottom Line Short Form – Environmental, Part 3

Water consumption and discharge amounts:

Policies and programs regarding water discharge quality:

Assessment of impact of operations and of goods or services impact on habitats and of programs to protect biodiversity:

CHAPTER 4

Marketing and Sales and Eco-Labels

For your information

A BILLBOARD OR SUPER BOWL AD. A tweet. Word-of-mouth. All of these are marketing. And much more.

The first ingredient to marketing is information. Add persuasion and you have marketing. Without marketing, there are no sales, and a business fails.

Marketing can be broken into five functions:[16]

- Creating value – innovation, customer experience, differentiation, extended life, partnerships.

- Delivering value – retail, online, catalogue, telephone, postal service.

- Communicating value – service, quality, variety, price.

- Selling – the techniques that lead to the exchange of money for product.

- Managing customer relationships – customer service, customer loyalty programs.

Before marketing, a company identifies its target market. The target market is the people or businesses that will buy from the company. The target marketing is then segmented by demographics, tastes and other proclivities.

Targets and segments

Another way to think of target markets is to consider the stakeholders. When looking at corporate governance, we defined stakeholders as those 'who can affect or [are] affected by the achievement of the organization's objectives'. Two questions arise: Who are your stakeholders? How are they affected by a company and how do they affect a company?

First, stakeholders. They include:

- Customers

- Shareholders

- Employees and managers

- Suppliers

- Competitors

- Financial institutions

- Partners

- Trade associations

- Labor unions

- Regulators and local authorities

- Local and national communities

- Media

- Not-for-profits, activists and watchdogs

- Public at large

- Others . . .

Second, how do they affect your business and how do you affect them? One way to understand how stakeholders – other than customers – affect your company is by classifying them into four categories:[17]

- Dolphins – creative, adaptable, learn quickly

- Sea lions – keen to please, mainstream, professional

- Orcas – strategic, independent, unpredictable

- Sharks – instinctual, tactical, attack-minded

Many businesses form alliances with stakeholders that are 'dolphins' and 'sea lions' to gain a competitive advantage. These alliances allow you to have an influence on how other stakeholders affect your customers – driving them to or away from your product. Eco-labels are the signal for many alliances.

Eco-labels: Does this mean you're green?

LEED for buildings, Forest Stewardship Council for wood, Energy Star for appliances, USDA Organic for foods, Fair Trade for coffee or chocolate, that recycled or recyclable arrowed-triangle for plastic or paper. These are just a few of over 400 eco-labels worldwide.[18]

Eco-labels tell customers that your product is certified to a set of standards. It takes about four months to obtain certification, and most certifications last for two years.[19] Most are voluntary.

When choosing an eco-label, you need to pay attention to three factors:[20]

1. Are the standards objective and meaningful?

2. Is the label used by the customer to differentiate your product based on an environmental, social or economic factor about which they care?

3. Are the standards legitimate and is the label validated?

Objectivity means that an eco-labeling organization is not influenced or potentially influenced by compromising forces such as through a funding source or board of director membership. Your stakeholders determine if an eco-label is meaningful.

Legitimacy means that the standards uphold the sustainability value they advertise. Validation means that the stakeholder you are working with has some way of making sure your company is adhering to the standards. Almost all eco-labels require some sort of certification. This may be through reporting of data, a site visit or the hiring of a third party. Without legitimacy and validation of your eco-label, you run the risk of accusations of greenwashing.

Greenwashing – Managing the risks

Greenwashing is using sustainability communications to deceive customers that a company is environmentally or socially friendly.[21] The jury is still out on whether customers can sue a company for false sustainability advertising under unfair competition laws.[22]

The US Federal Trade Commission 'Guides for the Use of Environmental Marketing Claims' sets out guidelines and gives helpful examples for risk management.[23] The European Commission 'EU Ecolabel' is one of the most robust and well respected eco-labels worldwide, and sets a strong example.[24]

Dolphins, sea lions and the eco-labels

When deciding which eco-labels to use, here are three steps:

1. Does your customer/stakeholder recognize the eco-label? If so, look for the competitive advantage the eco-label provides. If not, look for new target markets and ways to appeal to an unexplored customer base.

2. Is the stakeholder organization offering the eco-label a dolphin or sea lion rather than orca or shark? If the latter, look carefully at the history between other businesses and the eco-labeling organization. If a dolphin or sea lion, look carefully at the objectiveness and legitimacy of the standards.

3. Is there value added to your business performance in the validation and certification process? If so, look for ways to dovetail the process with sustainability activities on another station in the value chain. If not, carefully weigh the costs and perceived benefits and look for other eco-labels.

Eco-Label Graphic Matrix

You may decide to use more than one eco-label. Eco-labels may be on your website, your company pamphlets, your label or other marketing materials. How do you display them all in a way that gives you the greatest advantage and just plain makes sense? You have to put them in a context. For this purpose I have developed a tool called the Eco-Label Graphic Matrix.

....

FIGURE 6. Eco-Label Graphic Matrix

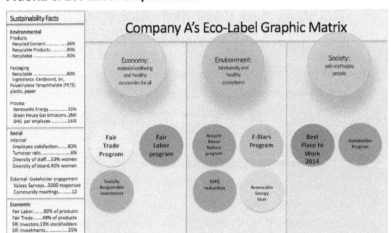

The Eco-Label Graphic Matrix is organized along the three areas of sustainability – economy, environment and society – and has fields for you to place your eco-labels. On the side is a factsheet arranged similarly to the ingredients label on foods.

Tips for use

You will need to determine the area for each eco-label, and decide how to communicate the facts so they are meaningful to your customers. If your company has many environmental eco-labels, but none or few social or economic labels, you can adapt the areas in the Eco-Label Graphic Matrix into aspects of the environment or group economy and society.

....

FIGURES 7. Adapted Eco-Label Graphic Matrix (two versions)

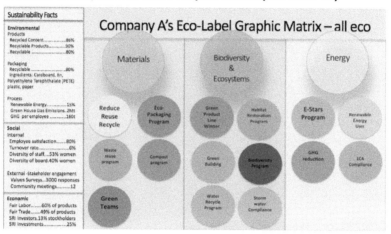

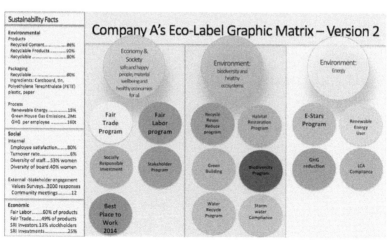

CHAPTER 5

Procurement and Natural Resource-Based Procurement

Direct and indirect

PROCUREMENT IS THE PURCHASING of goods and services. There are two types of procurement:

- Direct – used to produce a good: raw materials, semi-finished materials, parts.

- Indirect – used by people in the company: equipment, utilities, office supplies, maintenance services, consulting services (including for IT, HR, marketing, etc.).

It was not until after companies experienced long-term scarcity during World War II that procurement became a managerial rather than clerical function. With the forces of globalization and consolidation, procurement became a science.[25] In the last 20 years, political instability, the competitive environment and technological advances have had dramatic impacts on procurement practices.[26] Natural resource depletion is earmarked as the next wave to hit procurement.

Green procurement

Green procurement is the coupling of environmental and health measures with cost when purchasing. It is often done by classifying impacts for a type of product or service, sometimes in tandem with a life cycle analysis. Suppliers are then selected according to the green criteria, which includes cost savings in terms of money as well as measures such as greenhouse gas emission reduction, water usage rate decrease and waste reduction. The European Union provides sets of green procurement criteria for procurement of goods ranging from paper to food services.[27]

Stepping up

Many companies base their procurement on principles put forth by 'The Natural Step'.[28] These procurement policies list desirable and undesirable features, supplier activities – such as take-backs and recycling – and procurement options.[29] The first three principles of the Natural Step are focused on the environment and the fourth on society. They are summarized here:

1. Natural resources are used at or below the rate nature can replenish them, so that depletion of natural resources does not systematically increase over time.

2. Production levels do not systematically increase.

3. Pollution is generated at or below the rate nature can process it and restore the environment to a healthy status, so that pollution and degradation of nature does not systematically increase over time.

4. All people can meet their needs.

When crafting your procurement policies, you can use the Natural Step's principles to guide your criteria. For example:

- Organic, non-toxic, bio-degradable or compostable raw materials and semi-finished materials.

- Restored, recycled or recyclable parts or equipment.

- Equipment or services that reduce or eliminate use of natural resources, toxins or pollution generation.

- Raw materials, semi-finished materials or parts that are sourced in a way that supports people's capacity to meet needs.

A good practice is to form a policy for a set number of items procured and include specific criteria for each item. These can include eco-labels for suppliers, lists of toxins to avoid or chemical components to seek, as well as desirable supplier activities.

Sustainability ratios

Sustainable development ratios are used on a large scale by policy-makers to guide decisions.[30] Here I provide you with the Sustainability Ratio tool, which is designed to help you link your company's internal policies to the status of the environment, society or economy for your region.

It is up to you to define your region. For a manufacturing firm focusing on water resources, the region may be a province or county. For a retail firm focusing on human rights, the region may include countries where raw materials are sourced, the product is manufactured and the places of sale. For a small service company, the region may be a city or rural community.

You can use it on two levels. You can conduct a thorough analysis of the status of your region's sustainability in regards to the item you are procuring. You can also develop a sustainability strategy, complete with goals and metrics, for the items you procure. This way your understanding of your company's impact is grounded in facts. However, in some cases it may be difficult to gather information. You can also use this tool in a more general way, using guesstimates for your company and regional sustainability status. This tool is intended for internal use as a working process to understand the relationship between your procurement and sustainability. Below is an example of how the tool can be used and a tool ready for use.

....

FIGURE 8. Sustainability ratio examples

Procured item	Company's sustainability goal	Company's sustainability indicator	Regional sustainability indicator	Regional sustainability trend	Sustainability ratio
Water	Reduce water usage	Water consumption levels: 100K gal/day at company operations	Drinking water supply levels 45M gal/day in the city of company operations	Overall consumption trending down	100K: 45M gal/ day with a downward trend in consumption
Cotton fabric	Organic cotton	Percent of cotton procured that is organic: 10%	Percent of organic cotton market globally: 0.75%	Small but strong trend upwards in portion of cotton market that is organic	10% of company's cotton/ 0.75% of global cotton market that is organic with a small and strong trend upwards

Consulting services	Strong local economy	Portion of spending on locally owned businesses to all spending: 30% on local businesses in place of company operations	Increase in wages paid in the local economy that are spent in the local economy: 30M (10% of annual economy) in city of company operations	Weak increase in wages paid and spent economy	30% of consulting service budget on local business/ 10% of annual economy that is local business with a weak trend upward toward local economic strength

FIGURE 9. Sustainability Ratio Tool

Procured item	Company's sustainability goal	Company's sustainability indicator	Regional sustainability indicator	Regional sustainability trend	Sustainability ratio

CHAPTER 6

Operations and Life Cycle Analysis

Operations – Profit in the short term, profit in the long term

OPERATIONS KEEP A BUSINESS GOING. It is all about productivity, which entails three things:

1. Whatever is produced – goods or services – is more valuable than the resources that went into them.

2. Profitability is sustained.

3. Profit increases.

The granddaddy of management

Peter Drucker, the 'man who invented management', formulated the notion of 'management by objectives'.[31] The three principles of management by objectives are 1) goals are set, 2) an action plan is formed and 3) employees are given the level of decision-making power that allows them to fulfill the goal.[32]

The most important ingredient

Your people – from the guy at the loading dock to the vice president – are the most important asset of a company. Drucker taught the importance of investing in employees, whether 'blue collar' or 'knowledge' workers. He saw that productivity increases with increases in worker knowledge.[33]

Life cycle analysis and productivity

Sustainability means keeping the planet going. It is about positive outcomes for people, nature and businesses in the short and long term. One tool to do this is a life cycle analysis or 'LCA'.[34] LCAs were developed to measure and reduce costs to the environment. An LCA looks at impacts on each link of the supply chain for a product or service.

One of the first LCAs, called an 'Ecobalance', compared the total energy – the impact – used to produce glass, plastic, steel and aluminum beverage containers.[35] It was developed in the early 1970s. In the intervening years, LCAs became very complex, accounting for multiple impacts that only scientists could measure for every possible link in the supply chain.[36] Many companies became disenchanted, seeing LCA efforts as terrifically expensive analysis with little application.

Efficiency and life cycle analysis

An LCA can be used to reduce costs to the environment and the bottom line. Three guidelines for conducting an LCA are:

1. Keep it relevant.

2. Be dynamic.

3. Keep it simple.

On keeping it relevant, stakeholders are the key. Here is where you find out what process, product or service to measure. You need to know what is important to your stakeholders. For a manufacturing firm, a regulator may care about waste and toxins while managers are more concerned about energy use and recycled inputs. For a service company, clients may want you to manage paper and other supplies while employees may care about greenhouse gas emission and travel costs.

Be dynamic – stakeholders are still the key, and so are costs. Keep the dialogue open with your stakeholders. Interests change, particularly as we learn more. This means the impacts on your LCA may need to be adjusted. Include costs to produce per unit, so you can track and link environmental and financial costs. Think creatively about how measuring and managing an impact can reduce costs. Sometimes the connection is clear. This usually means increasing efficiency or reducing use. Sometimes it is less clear, and may mean a new approach or a change to a system.

Last and most importantly – keep it simple. You may end up with ten products, services or inputs to measure and 25 impacts. Bring it down to just a few – three or four, if you can. And when measuring, follow the adage 'perfection is the enemy of good'.[37] You may get as much from an LCA as a means to facilitate conversation and understand impacts as from the actual measurements.

Below is an adaptable approach for an LCA.

LCA Grid

The Life Cycle Analysis Grid integrates the goal of zero waste into the supply chain by adding the design of a product or service and its use, reuse or disposal. I call this the 'Zero Waste Supply Chain'.

FIGURE 10. The Zero Waste Supply Chain

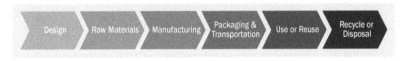

You can use the LCA Grid for one product or service, or to compare several products or inputs for a project. Below are examples of the LCA Grids used for analysis, one for the classic 'paper or plastic' bag decision – considering one plastic bag and one paper bag – the other for the environmental impacts of providing engineering consulting services. This chapter concludes with a blank LCA Grid for your use.

FIGURE 11. Paper or plastic bag LCA Grid

Life cycle analysis grid for a paper bag	Design	Raw materials	Manu-facturing	Packaging & trans-portation	Use or reuse	Recycle or disposal
Energy use Ttl energy 1629 BTU 0.1 GHG	29 BTU	300 BTU	1000 BTU	200 BTU	0 BTU	100 BTU
Waste	.		0.1 oz. GHG 2.5 gallons water			200 years to decompose in a landfill
Materials	n/a	1 bag is 0.14% of a tree, 30% of trees cut in the US are used for bags	0.1 ounces GHG per bag	.00058 gallons of diesel	Used 1.5 times on average	50% recycle rates recyclable 6 times max.

Cost to produce per unit: .26 cents

FIGURE 12. Plastic bag LCA Grid

Life cycle analysis grid for a plastic bag	Design	Raw materials	Manu-facturing	Packaging & trans-portation	Use or reuse	Recycle or disposal
Energy use	4 BTU	140 BTU	400 BTU	50 BTU	0 BTU	100 BTU
Ttl energy 694 BTU						
Waste	.		0.02 GHG per bag. 0.5 gallons water		Carries ¼ to ½ the amount of a paper bag	1000 years to decompose in a landfill
Materials	n/a	.000001 gallons of oil per bag, 0.17% of all oil used in the US	.02 ounces GHG per bag	,00006 gallons of diesel	Used once on average	1% recycle rates, indefinite recyclability

Cost to produce per unit: .204 cents

FIGURE 13. LCA Grid – example for service

Life cycle analysis grid for 40 hours of engineering consulting	Design	Raw materials	Manufacturing	Packaging & transportation	Use or reuse	Recycle or disposal
Paper	.	1000 pages of paper ($60 dollars)			Marketing materials: 50 pages glossy paper ($40 dollars)	
Energy and GHG emissions			Electrical Energy use per week of work: 243 kWh	0.33 metric tons GHG emissions (double average in US) ($200 gas costs per week)		

Total cost to product per hour: $77 per week: $3080

FIGURE 14. LCA Grid – for use

Life cycle analysis grid	Design	Raw materials	Manu-facturing	Packaging & trans-portation	Use or reuse	Recycle or disposal
Input 1						
Input 2						
Input 3						

Cost to produce per unit:

CHAPTER 7

A Case Study:
A Look at a Company in the
Goods Industry – Patagonia

PATAGONIA IS PERHAPS THE MOST frequently cited example of business sustainability. Let's look at why. Annual revenues tripled between 2008 and 2012 up to 540 million.[38] They employ about 1500 people.[39] The company got its start in the 1970s supplying mountain climbers with reusable hardware so climbers could leave less of a trace on cliffs. It is founded on an imperative of minimizing the environmental harm done from business. Its gross profit margin is one of the highest in the industry.[40]

FIGURE 15. Patagonia sustainability value chain activities

Corporate Governance/ Corporate Responsibility	Workplace Code of Conduct
Accounting/Triple Bottom Line Accounting	Footprint Chronicles
Marketing & Sales/Eco-Labels	Eco-Label Coalition and Customer Community
Procurement/Natural Resource Based Procurement	E-Fabrics

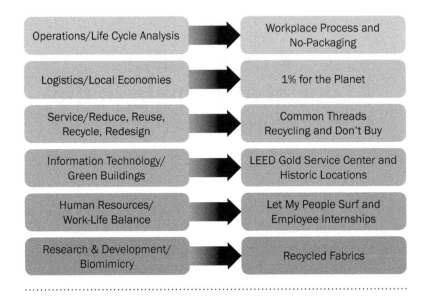

Operations/Life Cycle Analysis	Workplace Process and No-Packaging
Logistics/Local Economies	1% for the Planet
Service/Reduce, Reuse, Recycle, Redesign	Common Threads Recycling and Don't Buy
Information Technology/ Green Buildings	LEED Gold Service Center and Historic Locations
Human Resources/ Work-Life Balance	Let My People Surf and Employee Internships
Research & Development/ Biomimicry	Recycled Fabrics

Corporate governance and corporate responsibility

Corporate Governance/ Corporate Responsibility

From its early days, Patagonia aimed to be a model for other companies. Their mission statement reads 'Build the best product, cause no unnecessary harm, use business to inspire and implement solutions to the environmental crisis.' Its leadership is renowned for personally and professionally reflecting company values.[41]

The company's Workplace Code of Conduct has 14 principles that cover labor, human rights and environmental performance.[42] They are measured with a set of benchmarks.[43] The company reduced its number of suppliers by more than half between 2007 and 2012 in order to have the capacity to monitor for compliance with its code of conduct.[44] Supplier tracking charts are kept online by a non-profit.[45]

Accounting and the triple bottom line

Accounting/Triple
Bottom Line Accounting

Patagonia's Footprint Chronicles are an online interactive map that displays detailed information about supplier labor practices and environmental performance.[46] Patagonia's early Footprint Chronicles – issued in 2007 – tracked energy use, carbon footprint and raw materials of some of its products. In an effort towards greater transparency, in 2012 they transitioned to a supplier-focus.[47]

Marketing & sales and eco-labels

Marketing & Sales/Eco-Labels

Patagonia spearheaded the Sustainable Apparel Coalition, a group of companies and non-governmental, educational, trade and governmental agencies.[48] They are creating the Higg Index, the equivalent of a nutritional label for apparel that will display social and environmental impacts and allow apparel companies to manage these impacts.

Patagonia spends less than 1% of revenues on marketing.[49] It focuses on educating and inspiring customers to conserve and restore the environment and enjoy nature through their catalogues. They call their customers 'Patagoniacs' or 'Dirtbags' (extreme sports enthusiasts) and build community by sharing their stories and facilitating customer interactions.

Procurement/natural resource based procurement

Procurement/Natural
Resource Based Procurement

Patagonia was the first company to introduce fleece into the apparel market and helped invent it with Malden Mills.[50] They continued working with the company to produce the world's first fleece made from recycled plastic and now are creating fabric made from recycled clothing. They also spearheaded organic cotton clothing, hemp and recycled nylon clothing.

Operations and life cycle analysis

Operations/Life Cycle Analysis

Company planning is conducted through a process they call 'workbook', whereby employees from all levels participate in decisions. The life cycle analysis of each item is an ongoing effort and includes customers, suppliers and other stakeholders through the Footprint Chronicles as well as partnerships with bluesign Standard and the Fair Labor Organization, a non-profit that performs environmental and human rights audits of suppliers respectively. Most of their packaging has been eliminated and replaced by 'sushi' rolling garments and securing them with rubber bands.[51]

Logistics and local economies

Logistics/Local Economies

One percent of Patagonia's revenues are donated to conserve and restore nature. Each store has a budget that they are allowed to give to grassroots environmental groups in their area. The company also supports several international groups. They have given over $46 million in 27 years.[52] They started an international association, 1% For The Planet, in 2001 to encourage other businesses to donate 1% of sales to environmental causes. In 2012, there were 1200 member businesses in 38 countries.

Service and reduce, reuse, recycle, redesign

Service/Reduce, Reuse, Recycle, Redesign

The company ran a full-page ad in the *New York Times* (paper and online) that read 'Don't Buy This Jacket' on Black Friday, 2011.[53] It was part of a campaign effort to raise awareness of the impacts of consumerism on the environment and to encourage people to use, repair and reuse goods. People were encouraged to take the Common Treads Partnership pledge, promising to reduce consumption, repair and reuse products, recycle worn out gear giving it back to Patagonia, and reimagine a world where resources are used at the rate nature can replenish. Customers are encouraged to sell used items on their eBay storefront.

Information technology and green buildings

Information Technology/ Green Buildings

In the mid-1990s Patagonia moved its shipping center from the headquarters in Ventura, California to Reno, Nevada after a study to find a location with the lowest environmental impact from travel. The building is LEED Gold certified.[54] It is solar powered and uses an air-cooling system at night so there is no need for air-conditioning in the desert heat in the summer.[55] The building is made from recycled materials and recycling practices within the building leave only two dumpsters worth of garbage a year. Stormwater is managed with a pervious parking lot and underground filtration. It has over 50 outlets across the globe. The company tries to open stores in historic buildings in a way that preserves local culture and renovates using recycled and environmentally friendly products.[56]

Human resources and work–life balance

Human Resources/ Work-Life Balance

Flex-time is one of the tenets of the company. Stories of the early days of the company include staff and managers alike closing shop and heading to the beach when the surf was up. Employees are still encouraged to get into nature to test products as part of work. The company was one of the first to install a day-care facility in its headquarters, and serve organic food in its café. Benefits include paid sabbaticals for employees to intern at environmental non-profits and bail payment if arrested as an activist for an environmental cause.[57] About 900 people apply per opening.[58]

Research & Development/ Biomimicry
Research & development and biomimicry

Patagonia is developing clothing fabric made of garments that are no longer usable, mimicking natural systems in which there is no waste. In the early 1990s, they experimented with their 'Coat of Many Colors' program whereby scraps were made into clothing distributed by customers to people in need, often children, in developing nations.

CHAPTER 8

Logistics and Local Suppliers

Logistics: Right time, right place . . .

WARS HAVE BEEN WON AND LOST because of logistics. Cut off supply, and you bring your opponent to its knees. Logistics is 'having the right item in the right quantity at the right time at the right place for the right price in the right condition to the right customer'.[59] You can think of logistics as the arteries of the supply chain, ensuring everything flows smoothly so supply is possible. Figure 16 shows some of the functions of logistics.

On the value chain, operations are often sandwiched between inbound and outbound logistics. Inbound logistics is concerned with bringing everything it takes to make a product or service ready for sale – and use. Outbound logistics is concerned with getting the final product to the customer.

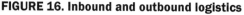

FIGURE 16. Inbound and outbound logistics

Logistics and sustainability

Logistics management is data-heavy and often software plays a major role. The main goal of logistics is reducing costs, followed by other goals such as increasing efficiency and quality and reducing waste.

Green logistics simply expands the goals set and data collected to include environmental and social impacts.[60] Some of the ways companies 'green' inbound and outboard logistics are:

1. Reducing pollution in transportation – greenhouse gases and other air emissions, noise and vibration.

2. Maximizing delivery vehicle utilization and fuel efficiency in transportation.

3. Increasing utilization of warehouse space, sharing marking and intermodal terminals.

4. Leasing or owning distribution centers and other logistics facilities in logistics zones to reduce sprawl.

5. Increasing safety, quality and product life in production, increasing density and reducing weight or size to reduce transportation costs.

6. Improving recycling and reducing waste after sales, reducing packaging and designing low density packaging from recycled content.

7. Preparing for adaptation of logistics systems in response to climate change, changes in customer behavior and regulations.

8. Increasing use of local suppliers and the local customer base.

Local economies

Logistics begins with procuring materials, or 'raw materials'. For most companies, these materials are procured from suppliers. Buying more from local suppliers and fostering business in a local region is a good way to integrate sustainability into your logistics.

In sustainability, 'local' is an important concept. This is because strong local economies lead to greater resilience economically and socially.[61] One of the major lessons from Japan's '3-11' event – a perfect storm of natural and human disasters with a tsunami, earthquake and nuclear meltdown – came from the breakdown in logistics.[62] As you buy more from local suppliers, the local economy gets stronger.[63]

The local multiplier

One reason buying locally makes a difference is the multiplier effect. The multiplier effect says that money spent by one person is income to the next person, who then goes out and spends the money they earned, which is income to a third person, and so on. A multiplier is calculated using the percentage of additional income people spend and save.[64] The equation is:

FIGURE 17. Multiplier equation

**The multiplier
=
1/(1- the percent of new income people spend)**

If in one city, people spend half their additional income and save half, the multiplier effect is 2, meaning for each dollar spent, 2 dollars of income is generated. If in another city, people spend 75% of their additional income, and save 25%, then for each dollar spent 4 dollars of income is generated.

Multipliers vary depending on where money comes from – business spending, government expenditure or fiscal policy changes – and the income levels of people who gain the new income. Calculating them can be difficult. A conservative estimate for the US is 1.4.[65] Because local multipliers are not easy to attain, you may need to communicate the benefits of increasing local suppliers in other ways.

The Local-Global Scorecard

The Local-Global Scorecard is a simple tool to help you to manage your local supplier-related business performance. You can use it internally as a decision tool or externally to communicate in a community, city or region.

First and foremost, you will need to define the term 'local' for your company. Some companies define 'local' in a geographical way, meaning 100 miles within a city or state, or even country. Others define 'local' in terms of relationship, meaning small businesses or farms.

In the section providing the number of local suppliers, you will need to determine your baseline and whether you will aim to increase or maintain the number of local suppliers or portion of budget for local supply. You can garner savings in miles by comparing the average miles traveled by non-local and local suppliers. You can gather the portion of budget or amount spent on local suppliers from your controller, and you may need

FIGURE 18. Global Local Scorecard

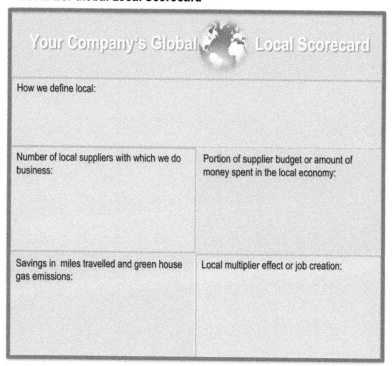

to use an estimate for the local multiplier effect or job creation in a local area. You can substitute any of these fields with others you feel are more relevant to your managers or your local customers.

CHAPTER 9

Service and Reduce, Reuse, Recycle

Customer service

SERVICE, MORE APTLY CUSTOMER SERVICE or technical support, is all the 'activities designed to enhance the level of customer satisfaction – that is, the feeling that a product or service has met the customer expectation'.[66]

Common business lore tells you that keeping customers happy is critical. Dissatisfied customers will more than likely talk about their negative experiences to an average of 11 people, while satisfied customers may tell up to four people.[67]

Customer service activities include:

- Touch-tone self-service

- Online automated support

- Call-in service

- In-person sales and service

- Cell phone apps designed for customer feedback

- Online, telephone or in-person surveys for customer feedback

- In-person installations, training and maintenance

- Maintenance support and services

- Return support

Where marketing ends and service begins

Marketing is all the activities that lead up to a sale. Customer service takes over after the sale. The two are inextricably linked through the sale. The sale is considered part of marketing, but is performed by employees providing service.

....

FIGURE 19. Marketing and sales

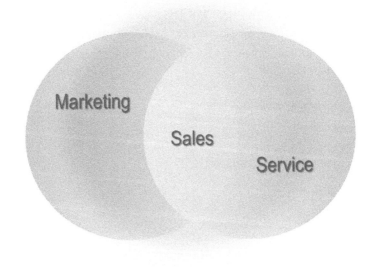

Customer service and sustainability

The primary objective of service is keeping your customer happy, now and in the future. The primary objective of sustainability is keeping our environment, society and economies healthy, now and in the future. More and more businesses are finding that putting these two priorities side-by-side – profit and sustainability – puts them 'ahead of the pack'.[68]

Businesses prioritizing customer service and sustainability can distinguish themselves from their competitors. Some of the ways companies do this are:[69]

1. For each purchase, planting a tree, donating a portion of proceeds, or providing another product made from recycled or by-product materials to a person living at or below poverty level.

2. Offsetting credit transactions such as carbon offsets for travel or investment in local communities or job creation for retail

3. Hosting educational or informative events for customers.

4. Partnering with non-profits to offer educational tools for customer sustainability efforts.

5. Partnering with non-profits or agencies to engage in volunteer-driven projects, sometimes with the projects acting to offset negative impacts of a company such as wetland restoration for mining, low income housing for construction, children's health services for fast food.

6. 'Tithing' or using a portion of profit or revenue for charitable donations or to fund sustainability related projects.

7. Using customer votes to determine which non-profits receive charitable donations.

8. Blogs and online forums for customers to discuss ideas and share concerns about social, environmental or economic concerns with the business.

9. Providing recycling options, reuse of products or coupons for future purchases with recycling.

Let's explore this last approach.

Reduce, reuse, recycle

FIGURE 20. Redesign, reuse, reduce, recycle

The icon for 'Reduce, Reuse, Recycle' is ubiquitous. You see it in the copy room in offices, as footers on emails, in many city streets, and on most packaging.

Recycling got a foothold in the US during World War II, when resources for civilian life became scarce due to the need to support the war. Prior to that, waste management was largely focused on human health and safety. This was because the lack of waste management had been a plague upon many cities and communities for centuries.[70]

The idea of reduce, reuse and recycle grew in the 1970s and became more popular as our awareness of the environment grew. In the 1980s, a trend started. Companies began to use these concepts to reduce the environmental impact in the design of their process and products.

Zero waste

'Zero waste' is the idea that from all the natural and human resources that go into the manufacture and use of products there is no waste.[71] In the 1970s a group of scientists modeled the sustainability of our planet using five trends:[72]

1. Natural resource use

2. Waste production

3. Production of goods and services

4. Food production

5. Population

They found that if we generated no waste, then our environment would sustain our lifestyles much longer. Waste includes everything we dispose of, our emissions into air and water and other forms of unused resources or by-products rendered unusable.

One way businesses incorporate zero waste is in their processes – making them more efficient, leaner and reducing or eliminating harmful impacts on the environment. Another way is through redesigning products or services.

The Redesign Card

The Redesign Card is a tool to help you consider how you can rethink and redesign your products or processes for zero waste. It can be used at any station on the value chain.

It is based on the three legs of sustainability – environment, society and economy. The first column gives, in broad-brush strokes, sources for inspiration, and the second presents a few ideas to build on. This is designed for you to copy, print and stow in a pocket or wallet and take out when musing about sustainability and your business.

FIGURE 21. The Redesign Card

The Redesign Card	Sources for sustainable inspiration: Where we are, where we can be	Springboard for sustainable services: What we can offer
Reduce *think of the environment*	*Where we are*: Using natural resources at a rate faster than can be replenished. Generating more waste than nature can reabsorb safely. *Where we can be*: Using natural resources restoratively. Using waste as inputs.	*For services*: Increase value by providing ways for customers to get more efficiency and durability out of products. *For products*: Increase life of product and customer loyalty through additional services, upgrades, trade-ins and buy-backs.
Reuse *think of society*	*Where we are*: Unfair labor practices – including child and slave labor fairly common in some industries. A sense of isolation and loss-of-community for many. *Where we can be*: All peoples can meet basic physical and emotional needs. Fair labor practices globally.	*For services*: Offer after-sales services that bring customers together. Allow customer-to-customer communication and provide a sense of community. *For products*: Offer recycled or refurbished products to the markets in developing countries or markets at and close to poverty-level. Explore sales channels that lead to small businesses flourishing.

| Recycle *think of the economy* | *Where we are*: Growing disparity between the rich and poor. Unemployment and underemployment common. | *For services*: Strengthening your workforce through education or professional development. Letting customers provide input as to what kind of development and education service workers could use. |
| | *Where we can be*: Equal opportunity for all people. Companies are stewards of people, the planet *and* profit. | *For products*: Personify or 'put a face on' the supply chain so customers know that a real person in good working conditions made the product. |

CHAPTER 10

IT and Green Building

IT is . . .

IMAGINE A WORLD WITHOUT TECHNOLOGY. You can't. Technology – art plus skill – is the application of knowledge.[73] Perhaps the use of fire was our first technological invention, or hauling water.

Now imagine a world without IT – or information technology. You probably don't want to. But you might be able to. And you may remember when computers were the size of houses, weighed 30 tons and mobile phones were the size of bricks and weighed up to 76 pounds.[74]

IT is the use of hardware and software to manage information.[75] Today, every business depends on IT, or more precisely: IS – information systems. IS allows business managers to do their job.

A few information systems are:

- Enterprise management systems – business process management, data analysis and planning support.

- Database management – storage, mining and extraction of data, intranets, systems for control, integrity and security of data.

- Decision support – inventories of data, information and knowledge, analytical processes that encompass various circumstances and assumptions, group decision support.

- Expert systems – artificial intelligence, logic programs.

- Search engines – directories, data mining, real-time information.

- Customer relationship management – transaction processing, customer service data and management.

- Office systems – office automation, office information.

- Global information systems – systems for global distribution, multi-national users on a system, global cooperation systems, data integration.

The world runs on IT

The agricultural revolution took thousands of years.[76] It was followed by the industrial revolution, which took hundreds of years. The Technology Revolution emerged in a few decades.[77] It changed everything – not just how we do business but also who we are. Sustainability, like technology, may be the next 'revolution'. Every revolution has phases, much like the phases of an industrial life cycle: introduction, growth, maturity, decline.

If we are in the midst of the next revolution – a sustainability revolution – then we are in the early stages, somewhere between introduction and growth. We can look at two common factors of the industrial and IT revolutions to understand how a movement is carried forward: transfer of knowledge and innovation. Taking the idea of steam power from textiles to transportation is one example of how transfer of knowledge fueled the industrial revolution. Examples of innovation in technology

FIGURE 22. Revolution life cycles

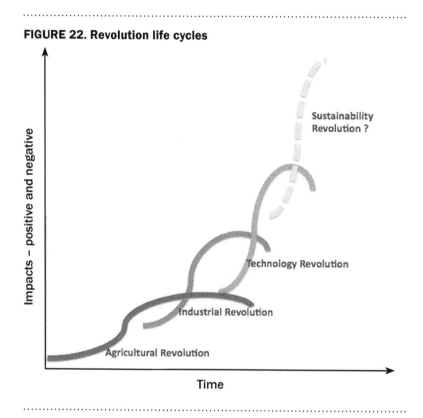

abound – from smart phones to chips so small and powerful they defy the imagination.

If sustainability is the revolution, one easy and obvious step forward that follows the lead of technology transfer and innovation is sustainability data management.

Sustainability and IS

Sustainable or 'green' IT usually takes three forms for businesses:[78]

- In the office, energy efficiency and waste reduction – energy savings, digital documents, hardware reuse or recycling.

- On the market, hardware that is less or non-toxic, has a longer lifetime, is reusable or easily upgraded.

- On the market, software programs that foster growth in sustainability markets.

A largely unexplored area is the management of sustainability data within an information system already used by a company, such as an enterprise management, database management or decision support system.[79] In this way, sustainability data would be collected alongside financial data, and managers can mine, analyze and manage sustainability as they can financial performance. As we discovered in Chapter 3, sustainably accounting gives us an understanding of what sort of data to capture.[80] Another place to look is the built environment.

Connecting the ephemeral and the concrete

The built environment is the physical space around us. Our buildings, roads, green spaces, water supply and energy systems are a few aspects of the built environment. Most people have heard of the LEED standards for buildings.[81] LEED is an eco-labeling program that defines 'green' building by establishing metrics. This is the place to start on what to measure, and manage, in the built environment.

Data centers are the ground zero of the built environment for every IT user.

The threats of climate change and demands for power outstripping supply have spurred an increase in the use of renewable energy and closed loop energy systems.[82] An example of the latter, gaining popularity in Europe, is district heating and cooling systems where surplus heat or coldness is recycled or used to warm or cool other areas rather than expelled.[83]

We explored three ways to green IT above. Below is a checklist for you to green your building, data center or other structure. It is modeled after LEED and follows the trends set by forward-thinking data center designers.

The Green IT Checklist

The Green IT Checklist is designed for use in an office, retail outlet, warehouse or other structure. On the left are activities and goals, and on the right column are categories of data for gathering.

Figure 23. The Green IT Checklist

ACTIVITIES AND GOALS	DATA TO GATHER
Energy	
Energy reduction and efficiency measures	Energy usage, emissions, costs and savings
Renewable energy	Energy reliability
Closed loop heat and cooling and heat island reduction	Energy investments and return

Water	
Water reduction and efficiency measures for building and landscaping	Water usage, discharge and costs
Closed loop water system for wastewater and rain	Water project investments and water discharge
Stormwater catchment and management	Stormwater investments and costs or savings
Materials	
Reuse and recycle management	Ratio of materials reused, recycled and reduced to materials sent to landfill, cost and savings for disposal
Waste reduction	
Renewable and/or non-toxic materials use	Materials investment and return
Health	
Access to views and daylight	Investment and productivity
Room temperature control	
Ventilation and access to healthy outdoor air	
Low emitting building materials and furniture	Investment, number of employee sick leave days and absenteeism
Indoor chemical and pollutant controls	

Nature	
Green space and access to nature on and near site(s)	Investment, diversity and number of plant and animal species, awards and accolades
Restoration and protection of habitat on and near site(s)	
Light pollution reduction on and near site(s)	
Community	
Mixed use and access to living quarters, food, healthcare and other amenities	Investment and employee satisfaction
Equal access to opportunities and resources	
Transportation	
Fleet – low emitting and fuel efficient	Investment, costs, savings and emissions
Access to public transportation	Employee commute patterns and emissions savings
Bicycle storage & showers	
Electric fuel car stations	
Commute time of employees	Employee time spent commuting

CHAPTER 11

Case Study: A Look at a Company in the Service Industry – One PacificCoast Bank

LET'S LOOK AT HOW A COMPANY in the service industry is integrating sustainability at every station on the value chain. One PacificCoast Bank is a small federal financial institution established in 2007. Among the 7092 banks in the US, it ranks 2197th in equity capital.[84] It has one of the highest loan growth rates among small banks.[85] The bank grew quickly between 2007 and 2012 through acquisition.

The bank's founders are a husband-and-wife team who were inspired to contribute towards the economics rights movement. The triple bottom line is the basis of all business performance.

....

FIGURE 24. One PacificCoast Bank sustainability value chain activities

Corporate Governance/ Corporate Responsibility	→	Beneficial Banking, Mission Reporting Statement
Accounting/Triple Bottom Line Accounting	→	Annual Beneficial Banking Report

Corporate governance and corporate responsibility

Corporate Governance/
Corporate Responsibility

The mission of One PacificCoast bank is 'to build prosperity in our communities through beneficial banking services delivered in an economically and environmentally sustainable manner'. Beneficial banking is defined through the bank's vision. The vision is a five-pronged approach to the banking industry, and acts as a code of conduct for the bank itself.[86] The five prongs are:

1. Fairness to the person with the least bargaining power.

2. Promotion of financial system stability.

3. Contribution to the sustainability of the environmental commons.

4. Access to financial services for all communities, particularly the traditionally under-served.

5. Long-term prosperity of responsible customers.

They track their performance toward these goals with an annual report, called the 'Beneficial Banking Report'. They also help borrowing companies to track their performance so the bank can understand the impact of their loans.

Accounting and the triple bottom line

Accounting/Triple
Bottom Line Accounting

In 2012, the bank issued its first triple bottom line report.[87] It is divided into three aspects: economic sustainability, social justice and environmental well-being. It includes the following sections:

1. Letter from founder: statement of bank's purpose, reporting principles, reporting goals and invitation for feedback.

2. Economic sustainability: key rations, balance sheet, income statement, quarterly loan growth.

3. Social justice and environmental well-being: mission-aligned lending, company practices, partners, bank operations: environmental sustainability, social justice outcomes, procurement policy and collective impacts.

The report was issued online. It includes past years' data for key ratios and greenhouse gas emissions. The diversity report covers employees but not governance. The report does not mention the Global Reporting Initiative's guidelines.

Marketing & Sales/Eco-Labels

Marketing & sales and eco-labels

The B-Corp eco-label can be found on the bank's website next to the Member FDIC label. They became a B-Corp in 2012.[88] B-Corp is a certification scheme based on an assessment that rates businesses on economic, social and environmental performance on a scale of 0–200 every two years. Random audits are performed on 10% of businesses annually. A business must have a score of at least 80 to carry the label. The company's score was 152 out of 200, one of the highest scores among the B-Corps's mid-sized companies.[89] Next to the B-Corp label can be found the Global Alliance for Banking on Values.[90] Under this scheme, the company promises to adhere to a set of principles and meet three criteria.

Procurement/Natural
Resource Based Procurement

Procurement/natural resource based procurement

The procurement policy is posted online, as part of its sustainability report, so that other companies can use it. It covers conservation of office materials and travel, selection of eco-friendly socially conscious suppliers and recycling guidelines.

Operations/Life Cycle Analysis

Operations and life cycle analysis

The company's Green House Gas Inventory includes 'scope 1, 2 and

3 activities' – meaning they include performance they have complete control over and they can only influence. Emissions are broken down by office and graphed over time per full-time employee.

Logistics and local economies

Logistics/Local Economies

The company's loan policies are designed to support strong local economies, with nine target markets. Nine percent of loans support neighborhood stabilization, 19% on low-income community economic development and 6% support the creation of affordable housing.[91] Eighty-three percent of loans are aligned to their mission.

Service and reduce, reuse, recycle, redesign

Service/Reduce, Reuse, Recycle, Redesign

All of the bank's profits go to a foundation, the One PacificCoast Foundation. The foundation funds services including training, workshops, events, awards programs, local business gift cards, an online marketplace and homeownership loan assistance that aim to foster community strength. The bank also provides a credit card, the Salmon Nation Visa, whereby a portion of income funds restoration of salmon habitat along the Pacific coast.[92]

Information technology and green buildings

Information Technology/ Green Buildings

Of the four offices the company maintains, two comply with LEED standards, one is built to be green and the other is certified by a local green business program.[93]

Human Resources/ Work-Life Balance

Human resources and work-life balance

Total employees amount to 56. The workforce reflects the gender and racial diversity of the US. Employee benefits run from medical, dental and life insurance, paid holidays and sick leave to wellness programs, tuition reimbursement and incentive/bonus programs. Employees are selected based on technical skill, their fit with the company's values, and whether the work fulfils their personal and professional goals.

Research & Development/ Biomimicry

Research & development and biomimicry

The connection that One PacificCoast Bank makes between financial and economic performance with environmental health and social justice is inherently based on natural systems. From the services this company offers to office supply practices, the company is informed by natural systems.

CHAPTER 12

Human Resources and Work-Life Balance

Human resources

HUMAN RESOURCES (HR) MANAGEMENT encompasses attracting, recruiting, hiring, training, developing, retaining, appraising and rewarding (or disciplining) employees. An HR department may also be responsible for negotiating with labor unions, health and safety, ensuring compliance with labor laws, and stewardship of the company culture. The measurements used by HR include employee turnover, compensation, productivity, grievances and employee satisfaction and diversity.[94]

In the next three sections, we list sustainability practices you can implement or expand upon in your HR department.

The sustainability already in HR: Training and education

Training is a basic human resources task. Sustainability precepts ask a company to invest more in their employees for the good of the company and the employee's well-being.

Below are ways you can integrate sustainability into training.

Training-related sustainability practices:

- Ongoing access to training for a job, professional development for promotion and mentoring for all levels of employees.

- Promotion of employees within the firm to middle and upper management.

- Education and care programs for those employed in the supply chain to ensure basic needs are met.

Green teams

Green teams are informal or formal groups of people within an organization, often from every level, who are motivated to implement sustainability practices in their office or company line of goods or services.[95]

They are often instrumental to successful integration of sustainability for a company.[96]

Steps to getting your green team going:

- Establish a time for people to meet on a weekly or monthly basis within departments or geographic regions.

- Set parameters and suggest goals but allow green teams to determine their own goals and metrics for measuring success.

- Allocate resources and/or allow green teams to change practices that are cost-effective such as suppliers, waste and recycling, car rental and travel.

- Provide communication tools to share best practices and lessons learned within the company, communicate green team successes to all in the company, and externally if it helps the company brand and reputation.

- Appoint a director or manager of sustainability or allocate responsibility for a current employee. Often someone is eager for this role within a company.

Diversity and equal opportunity

Diversity and equal opportunity are aspects of compliance with labor laws. In some firms, this is the responsibility of the legal department. Most companies take a proactive approach to their staffing. Research shows that a more diverse workforce has a positive impact on profits, but it is critical to prepare and educate people to gain from the benefits.[97]

Measures you can take to gain the benefits of diversity in your company:

- Adopt a clear and simply stated policy for diversity and inclusion.

- Set goals and measure outcomes for inclusion at all levels in the workplace: staff, management and governance/the board.

- Issue an annual diversity and inclusion report.

- Appoint a social justice position to guide staff management and product decisions.

- Provide anti-racism education and cultural sensitivity training for all. This can be introduced online and in pamphlets, then in sessions with trained professional facilitators.

- Increase team-building exercises and foster employee camaraderie such as happy hours after work, potluck lunches and other activities to develop sense of cohesiveness in departments and on teams as they become more diverse.

- Offer goods or services that foster and support cultural diversity in the marketplace.

- Collaborate with other companies to mend social injustice along the supply chain and in the market place.

Health and safety

Oftentimes, health and safety programs are focused on compliance and so lose the potential higher profits linked to safer working environments and healthier employees. Emerging research indicates that a healthier workforce is directly tied to higher profits.[98]

Sustainability related health and safety activities:

- Zero injury goals for industrial or hazardous workplaces.

- Ideas teams made up of employees working under the conditions of concern. Regularly solicit for ideas, act upon them, track impacts and recognize and reward employees for ideas that increase safety and profit.

- Design wellness programs for behavior changes by ensuring services are provided to all employees – from the fit to those with chronic health conditions – and by providing financial or other incentives for participating, through clear and consistent communication within the company, and by gathering input from employees about what wellness programs they desire, and by measuring the outcomes from the programs.

- Employ a wellness leave program whereby employees with accrued sick leave are compensated with 'wellness leave' – allowing employees to take sick leave days for physical or mental fitness activities.

- Employ wellness programs such as personal coaches for the employee and their spouse for stress, weight, email or time management, provide on-site exercise facilities or access to a nearby health club, provide mindfulness training.

- Adopt work–life balance policies and programs such as on-site childcare, flextime, job sharing, compressed work-weeks, allowing for alternative work sites and telecommuting.

- Adopt a code of conduct for labor practices and human rights on the supply chain.

Work–life balance

There is a lot of buzz about work–life balance. The term is usually used to describe a trade-off between work and living life. However, for most of us, work is an important part of life, even defining who we are, not something we balance against life. The Balanced Scorecard for Life is a tool that you can provide to your staff to help them define work–life balance for themselves. It is most helpful as a contemplative measure.

It is based on the Balanced Scorecard, a tool developed by Kaplan and Norton to help companies implement their mission and strategy.[99] It owes its history to dashboards used by process engineers seeking to manage chemical reactions and the popularity of performance measurements in the 1950s.

Where your company has a mentor program, the scorecard can be used for professional development. Managers can use it to define work–life balance for their company and which sustainability activities fit the company needs and culture.

Values

Before using the tool, it is important to define your personal values. Your values are what is important to you, what inspires you, what you believe in. Your values guide you in your decisions: how you spend your time, what you do for your work, with your family and friends and for fun.

The eighteenth-century American polymath Benjamin Franklin once identified all his values.[100] He found he had 13, listed below:

- Temperance: Eat not to dullness; drink not to elevation.

- Order: Let all your things have their places; let each part of your business have its time.

- Resolution: Resolve to perform what you ought; perform without fail what you resolve.

- Frugality: Make no expense but to do good to others or yourself; i.e. waste nothing.

- Moderation: Avoid extremes; forbear resenting injuries so much as you think they deserve.

- Industry: Lose no time; be always employed in something useful; cut off all unnecessary actions.

- Cleanliness: Tolerate no un-cleanliness in body, clothes, or habitation.

- Tranquility: Be not disturbed at trifles, or at accidents common or unavoidable.

- Silence: Speak not but what may benefit others or yourself; avoid trifling conversation.

- Sincerity: Use no hurtful deceit; think innocently and justly, and, if you speak, speak accordingly.

- Justice: Wrong none by doing injuries, or omitting the benefits that are your duty.

- Chastity: Rarely use venery but for health or offspring, never to dullness, weakness, or the injury of your own or another's peace or reputation.

- Humility: Imitate Jesus and Socrates.

He regularly assessed himself according to his values on paper. He also focused on one value for a week, and tried to live according to it. Lore has it that a friend pointed out that humility was not listed as one of his values. He added this, then tried to live by it for a week, found it was not really one of his values. His solution was to redefine humility, a somewhat ironic approach.

These are Ben Franklin's values. Other values you may have are:

- Achievement
- Accountability
- Adventure
- Ambition
- Beauty
- Bravery
- Calm
- Caring
- Challenge
- Community
- Competency
- Competition
- Cooperation
- Courage
- Collaboration
- Creativity
- Dependability

- Dignity
- Discipline
- Efficiency
- Energy
- Excellence
- Excitement
- Flexibility
- Freedom
- Generosity
- Helpfulness
- Honesty
- Independence
- Individuality
- Integrity
- Innovativeness
- Harmony
- Imagination

- Integrity
- Intelligence
- Justice
- Learning
- Loyalty
- Love
- Peace
- Persistence
- Quality
- Respect
- Responsibility
- Quiet
- Serenity
- Sincerity
- Tranquility
- Truth
- Wisdom

Getting to your values

To identify your values, you can start by making a list like Benjamin Franklin did. If you are having a hard time, think about what angers or upsets you. What is upsetting? The unfairness or the injustice? Then justice or equity may be your value. Laziness or waste? Then productivity or efficiency may be your value. Meanness or stupidity? Then kindness or intelligence may be your value.

Try to identify at least three to five values before you use the Balanced Scorecard for Life.

The Balanced Scorecard for Life

The steps to use the Balanced Scorecard for Life are:

1. Identify your core values.

2. Draw the balanced life scorecard (see below). It contains four quadrants in life, but is a flexible tool. If you feel you have more or other ways to describe the areas of your life, define your own scorecard. Write your core values in the center of the balanced scorecard.

3. List all the activities in your life on small sticky-notes.

4. Place the activities on the scorecard with those activities that are most aligned to your values close to the center, and those not at all aligned on the outside of the scorecard.

5. Now take the time to contemplate where you spend most of your time and how this aligns with what you value in your life. Think

about how to do more of what is closest to your values and less of what is further from them. Think about the balance of activities and time spent on activities in the areas of your life.

....

FIGURE 25. The Balanced Scorecard for Life

Note the four quadrants: work, friends & family, community and alone time. You can redefine the quadrants for your life, if these do not fit.

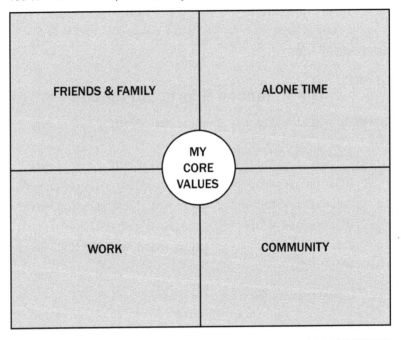

FIGURE 26. An example of the Balanced Scorecard for Life in use

Note this person placed the weekly conference calls, serving on a board of directors, house renovation project and journal writing on the outside or close to the outside of the quadrants. These are activities that are likely to cause this person stress and which they may be able to remedy by trading responsibilities at home, by delegating or by changing their career path to includes fewer of the activities they do not like and more of those they do enjoy.

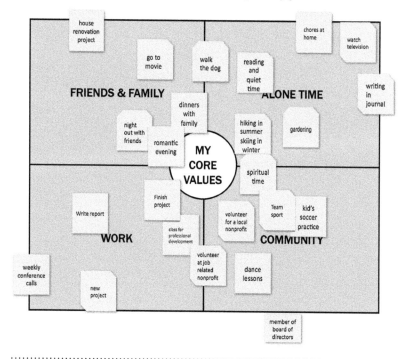

CHAPTER 13
R&D and Biomimcry

Research & development

RESEARCH & DEVELOPMENT (R&D) is where new products or processes are created, existing products are improved or updated, new markets are

....

FIGURE 27. The R&D path

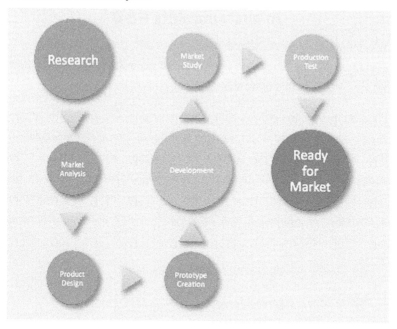

....

created, or markets restructured. During the research phase, information gathered from the marketing department is analyzed, a new product or process is designed and a prototype created. During the development phase, the product is tested on the production floor and through market studies.

Most companies dedicate a relatively small portion of their budget to R&D, except for those in the pharmaceutical, renewable energy, electronics and technology industries, where a large portion of the budget can go to R&D.[101]

Where the rubber meets the road in sustainability R&D

Two emerging markets where the process and product clearly fit with sustainability are renewable energies and ecosystem services.[102] Here we look at snapshots of what is happening in these markets.

Ecosystem services provide that which sustains and fulfills human life. Breathable air, clean water, healthy soil, food, fuel, climate regulation, flood control, outdoor recreation and connection with nature are a few ecosystem services. Although this emerging market is mostly in the research phase and much of the research is conducted by government agencies, it is interesting and inspiring. Some of the research being conducted includes:

- Wildfire management and fuel production

- Naturally replenishing soil health and agriculture

- River thermal systems and fish hatcheries

- Oyster habitat restoration and food service business

The renewable energy market is often talked about in conjunction with sustainability, because of the clear need for energy to sustain our lifestyles and the level of impact energy use is having on our climate. Some of the more innovative and newer forms of renewable energy are:

- District heating whereby heat discharged from one site is used to warm another site, such as steam piped from a manufacturing firm to a school.

- Use of business byproducts for energy sources, such as whey from dairies converted to fuel.

- Use of agricultural, industrial, garbage and human waste to create fuel and/or fertilizer.

- Artificial synthesis to create fuel and consume carbon.

Biomimicry

Biomimicry is the study and emulation of nature for purposes of business (as well as other organizations). The term was coined by Janine Benyus who explains that '(t)he core idea is that nature has already solved many of the problems we are grappling with: energy, transportation, climate control, food production, collaboration . . .'[103]

There are three levels of biomimicry:

- Natural form – The product you offer is based on an idea from nature rather than just using natural raw materials.

- Natural process – The business activities to bring a product to market – the value chain – are based on natural systems and do no harm to people or natural systems.

- Natural ecosystem – Your business sustains nature and people and fosters a shift in how other companies do business for a healthier environment and society.

Below are some examples of biomimicry products and processes:

- Gecko tape is a directional adhesive made of miniscule flexible hairs with split ends that interact with the molecules of the surface it is attached to, and is being used underwater and on space stations.

- Self-healing plastics, mimicking our bodies' ability to heal are made of hollow fibers filled with epoxy resin. If the surface is broken, the epoxy resin reseals the tear. It is being used in aircraft and space stations.

- Drag-reducing surfaces based on sharkskin are being used on ship hulls, submarines, aircraft and swimwear to reduce resistance.

- Canes for the blind use ultrasound (in daylight or the dark) in the same way bats do and send a signal if something is overhead, in front or to the side of the user.

- Flexible robotic arms are expandable and compressible like an elephant's trunk, with positional grips that can lift and turn heavy objects.

The Biomimcry Backwards Forwards Tool

The Biomimicry Backwards Forwards Tool helps you put your product and process line in the context of nature. You can use it for orienting employees or consulting towards sustainability, for brainstorming, or as a guide for research.

The aim is to develop the new technologies to meet future needs. It is also to find ways to meet the needs and demands of the marketplace today without compromising the ability of future generations to meet their needs. The tool is composed of three simple questions to ponder or provide to scientists and technicians in your R&D department.

FIGURE 28. The Biomimicry Backwards Forwards Tool

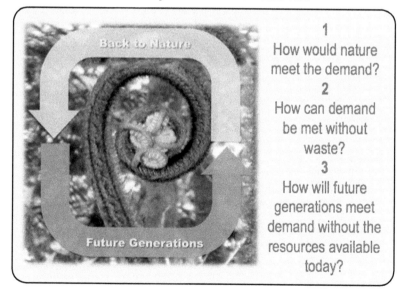

1
How would nature meet the demand?
2
How can demand be met without waste?
3
How will future generations meet demand without the resources available today?

CHAPTER 14

Conclusion

On change

THIS BOOK OFFERS YOU NINE TOOLS and many sustainability practices for use along your company's value chain. Change, no matter how small, is frightening to some and challenging to all. When you are implementing sustainability activities at your company, you are making a change. You can use the following tactics and principles, whether for a radical or incremental change.

Three tactics

The three tactics in managing the integration of sustainability are:

- Change only that which needs to be changed.

- Communicate consistency and in terms of risk rather than gain.

- Establish principles for the change.

The first tactic – change only that which needs to be changed – is about consistency. Keep everything that you do not change constant. People generally feel better when there is consistency. Also, by not changing other factors and areas of performance, you can better measure the impact of your change.

Here are some examples. When asking the operations department to track and manage greenhouse gas emissions, try to integrate the drivers for emissions into the current tracking system before putting in a new system. When factoring sustainability into purchasing decisions, where possible, keep the same supplier and delivery schedule. When adopting a sustainability program, craft a policy for sustainability that fits with your organization's current vision and mission.

The second tactic is about communication. Clearly communicate what will be changed and what will not be changed. Also, communicate the rationale for the change in terms of risk of loss if no change is made before talking about potential for gain. People are more likely to accept change if they fear they will otherwise lose something than if they hope to gain something by the change.

A third tactic is to establish clear principles for any change. Principles act as signposts. For those who disagree, challenge the change or become confused, principles can help soothe and guide the way.

Below are three principles you can use to guide your sustainability activities:

- The Profitability Principle – Businesses can provide the solutions to sustainability problems and not only make a profit but even increase profitability.

- The Integration Principle – Integrating tried and true sustainability activities into tried and true business practices is the path to a healthy environment, society and economy for all.

- The Incremental Principle – Sustainability is inherently an incremental process. Every step counts, and with each step, the path forward becomes clearer.

These tactics are applicable at any stage of implementing sustainability activities into all the value chain activities of your business. They can be applied when taking the first step or for a business known for its sustainability program.

It's not easy being green

Sustainability practices are, at their very core, simple common sense. At home, it's doing things your grandparents or great-grandparents took for granted, like reusing the glass milk bottle and not wasting. At work, it's doing business in a way that does no harm to people, communities or the environment – and even doing good.

But just because sustainability is simple, it does not mean it is easy. This is because today, we do not live in a sustainable world. Every business that practices sustainability is going against the grain of today's norm and will face challenges in finding the sweet spot between sustainability and profit. A time will come when sustainability practices will be the norm, and by employing the practices in this book, you position your company for the time when being green is easy.

Notes and References

1. Porter, M. 1985. *Competitive Advantage: Creating and Sustaining Superior Performance* (New York: The Free Press).

2. Freeman, R.E. 1984. *Strategic Management: A Stakeholder Approach* (Boston, MA: Cambridge University Press); Freeman, R.E. 2004. The OECD principles of corporate governance. In *OECD Better Policies for Better Lives*. Available at **www.oecd.org/dataoecd/32/18/31557724.pdf**.

3. Henriques, A. 2012. *Making the Most of Standards* (Oxford: DōSustainability); Kriton, J. and Trebilcock, M. 2004. *Hard Choices and Soft Law in Sustainable Global Governance* (London: Ashgate Publishers Ltd).

4. EU. 1998. On EU standards for European Enterprises operating in developing countries: Towards a European Code of Conduct. *European Code of Conduct (Final A4-0508/1998, PE 228.198/fin)*. Available at **http://www. europarl.europa.eu/sides/getDoc.do?type=REPORT&reference=A4-1998- 0508&language=EN**.

5. OECD. 2001/6. Codes of Corporate Conduct: Expanded Review of their Contents an OECD Working Paper on International Investment. Available at **http://www. oecd.org/dataoecd/57/24/1922656.pdf**.

6. Davidsson, P. 2002. Legal enforcement of corporate social responsibility within the EU. *Columbia Journal of European Law* (Volume 8): 529–535, citing *European Parliament, Committee on Development and Cooperation, Report on EU Standards for European Enterprises Operating in Developing Countries: Towards a European Code of Conduct (Final A4-0508/1998, PE 228.198/fin)*.

7. Picciotto, S. 2004. Rights, responsibilities and regulation of international business. *Columbia Journal of Transnational Law* (Volume 42, Number 1): 131, 141–144.

8. Links to the codes of conduct:

   OECD Guideline for Multinational Enterprises at **www.oecd.org/dataoecd/56/36/1922428.pdf.**

   Principles for Global Corporate Responsibly: Benchmarks at **www.bench-marks.org/downloads/Bench%20Marks%20-%20full.pdf.**

   UN Global Compact at **www.un.org/Depts/ptd/global.htm.**

   Caux Principles for Business at **www.cauxroundtable.org/principles.html.**

   Global Sullivan Principles at **http://www1.umn.edu/humanrts/links/sullivan principles.html.**

   CERES Principles at **www.ceres.org/coalitionandcompanies/principles.php.**

   ICC Business Charter for Sustainable Development at **www.bsdglobal.com/tools/principles_icc.asp.**

   Human Rights Principles and Responsibilities for TNCs and Other Business Enterprises at **www.unhchr.ch/huridocda/huridoca.nsf/(Symbol)/E.CN.4.Sub.2.2003.12.Rev.2.En.**

   ISO 26000 at **http://www.iso.org/iso/home/standards/iso26000.htm.**

9. Bantekas, I. 2004. Corporate social responsibility in international law. *Boston University International Law Journal* (Volume 22): 309–319.

10. The Benchmarks 8 step process that includes fashioning codes of conduct based on its principles. Benchmark's Simple Process:

    • Start off with principles that spell out a company's philosophy.

    • Engage stakeholders and redefine principles.

    • Agree on what issues are priorities and draw up policy that sets standards of expected company performance in these areas.

    • Put these into a code of conduct for each area of focus.

- Use the Bench Marks to guide and measure performance of policy and practice. This can be done incrementally by agreement with stakeholders as long as this does not contradict any local, national or international laws, treaties and conventions.

- Continually review progress and implementation and decide on further action.

- Use the Bench Marks Principles for public reporting.

11. Corporate Register. 2012. Global winners and reporting trends. Available at **www.corporateregister.com/a10723/45590-12th-11762220C1759774000T-GI.pdf.**

12. Karim, K. and Rutledge, R. 2004. *Environmental Disclosure Practices and Financial Performance* (Westport, CT: Greenwood Publishing Group).

13. The Global Reporting Initiative guidelines can be found online at www.global reporting.org/resourcelibrary/G3-Guidelines-Incl-Technical-Protocol.pdf.

14. Musikanski, L. 2012. *How to Account for Sustainability* (Oxford: DōSustainability).

15. Deming, E. 1993. *The New Economics for Industry, Government, Education* (Cambridge, MA: MIT Press).

16. American Marketing Association, 2007. Definition of marketing, at **www.marketingpower.com/aboutama/pages/definitionofmarketing.aspx** (defining marketing as 'the activity, set of institutions, and processes for creating, communicating, delivering, and exchanging offerings that have value for customers, clients, partners, and society at large').

17. The Global Compact. The 21st century NGO in the market of change. Available at **www.erb.umich.edu/News-and-Events/MayConferenceReading/21st_ngo.pd.**

18. EcoLabel Index. Available at **www.ecolabelindex.com/.**

19. World Resource Institute. 2010. Global 2010 EcoLabel Monitor 2010. Available at **www.ecolabelindex.com/downloads/Global_Ecolabel_Monitor2010.pdf.**

20. Golden, J. 2012. An overview of ecolabels and sustainability certifications in the global market place. Nicolas Institute for Environmental Policy Solutions at Duke University (Interim Report – Document #2012-10-1). Available at **http://center. sustainability.duke.edu/sites/default/files/documents/ecolabelsreport.pdf.**

21. Romero, P. 2008. Beware of green marketing, warns Greenpeace exec. *ABC. CBN.net.* Available at **www.abs-cbnnews.com/special-report/09/16/08/beware-green-marketing-warns-greenpeace-exec.**

22. The Oyez Project at IIT Chicago-Kent College of Law. 2003. Nike Inc. v. Kasky. Available on page 11 at **http://www.oyez.org/cases/2000-2009/2002/2002_02_575.**

23. Federal Trade Commission. FTC's guides for the use of evaluating environmental marketing. Available at **www.ftc.gov/bcp/grnrule/guides980427.htm.**

24. European Commission. 2012. EU Ecolabel. Available at **http://ec.europa.eu/ environment/ecolabel/.**

25. Brumer, I. 2012. A brief history of procurement: Golden ages past to come. *Procurement Intelligence Unit.* Available at **http://www.procurement-iu.com/ blog/2012/2/a_brief_history_of_procurement_golden_ages_past_and_to_ come.**

26. Kraljic, P., 1983. Purchasing must become supply management. *Harvard Business Review* (Volume 61, Number 5): 109–117.

27. European Commission. 2011. *Buying Green! A Handbook on Green Public Procurement.* Available at **http://ec.europa.eu/environment/gpp/buying_ handbook_en.htm.**

28. Robert, K. 2002. *The Natural Step: Seeding a Quiet Revolution* (Gabriola Island, BC: New Society Publishers).

29. Whistler ski resort is an example of a procurement policy based on the Natural Step. Available at **http://www.whistler2020.ca/whistler/site/product Assessment.acds?context=2065129.**

30. Micu, C. et al. 2010. The analysis of sustainable development ratios. *Annals, Economic Science Series* (Issue XVI): 731–737. Available at **http://fse.tibiscus. ro/anale/Lucrari2010/125.%20Micu%20Cristina.pdf**.

31. See about Peter Drucker on the *Harvard Business Review* website. Available at **http://hbr.org/authors/drucker**.

32. Drucker, P. 1954. *The Practice of Management* (New York: Harper & Row Publishers).

33. Drucker, P. et al. 2008. *The Five Most Important Questions You Will Ever Ask About Your Organization* (San Francisco, CA: Leader to Leader Institute).

34. LCA is also called Life Cycle Assessment or Life Cycle Inventory.

35. European Environmental Agency. 2006. *Life Cycle Assessment: A Guide to Approaches, Experiences and Information Sources* (Environmental Issues Services, Number 6). Available at **www.eea.europa.eu/publications/GH-07-97.../ Issue-report-No-6.pdf**.

36. Esty, D. and Simmons, P. 2011. *The Green to Gold Business Playbook* (Hoboken, NJ: John Wiley & Sons).

37. Voltaire. 1772. *La Bégueule – Conte Moral*. Originally published by the Bavarian State Library.

38. Martin, H. 2012. Outdoor retailer Patagonia puts environment ahead of sales growth. *Los Angeles Times*. Available at **http://articles.latimes.com/2012/ may/24/business/la-fi-patagonia-20120525**.

39. Gordon, C. 2012. Patagonia is hiring now: The inside scoop on getting a job. *Aol Jobs*. Available at **http://jobs.aol.com/articles/2012/08/10/patagonia-is-hiring-now-the-inside-scoop-on-getting-a-job/**.

40. Reinhardt, F. et al. 2011. Patagonia. Harvard Business School (9-711-020).

41. Knowledge at Wharton – 10,000 Women. 2009. Leadership, Patagonia-style: Changing the criteria for success. Available at **http://knowledge.wharton. upenn.edu/10000women/article.cfm?articleid=6032**.

42. Patagonia's Code of Conduct. Available at http://www.patagonia.com/pdf/en_US/CoC_English.pdf.

43. Patagonia's Social Responsibility Benchmarks. Available at http://www.patagonia.com/pdf/en_US/Code_of_Conduct_Benchmarks.pdf.

44. Patagonia. 2012. Patagonia clothing: Made where? How? Why? Available at http://www.thecleanestline.com/2012/04/patagonia-clothing-made-where-how-why.html.

45. Fair Labor Association Affiliate Patagonia Tracking Charts. Available at http://www.fairlabor.org/affiliate/patagonia.

46. Patagonia's Footprint Chronicles. Available at http://www.patagonia.com/us/footprint/.

47. Fogelson-Teel, M. 2012. Patagonia boosts corporate transparency with revamped "Footprint Chronicles" website. Ecouterre. Available at http://www.ecouterre.com/patagonia-boosts-corporate-transparency-with-revamped-footprint-chronicles-website/.

48. Patagonia. 2013. Working towards responsible supply chains: Our factory monitoring efforts. Clothesline. Available at http://www.thecleanestline.com/2013/05/working-towards-responsible-supply-chains-our-factory-monitoring-efforts.html. Access the Higg Index available at http://www.apparelcoalition.org/.

49. Reinhardt, F. et al. 2011. Patagonia. Harvard Business School (9-711-020).

50. Greenbaum, H. and Rubinstein, D. 2011. The evolution of fleece, from scratchy to snuggie. New York Times Magazine. Available at http://www.nytimes.com/2011/11/27/magazine/fleece-scratchy-to-snuggie.html?_r=0.

51. Patagonia. The Footprint Chronicles, BaseLayer Packaging: The good and the bad. Available at http://www.patagonia.com/pdf/en_US/packaging_info1.pdf.

52. Patagonia. 1% for the planet. Available at http://www.patagonia.com/us/patagonia.go?assetid=81218 and information about the organization One Percent for the Planet. Available at http://www.onepercentfortheplanet.org/en/.

53. *Marketing Week*. 2013. Case study: Patagonia's 'Don't buy this jacket' campaign. Available at http://www.marketingweek.co.uk/trends/case-study-patagonias-dont-buy-this-jacket-campaign/4005451.article.

54. *PR Newswire*. Patagonia received Green Building Council's Gold Certification honor. Available at http://www.prnewswire.com/news-releases/patagonia-receives-green-building-councils-gold-certification-honor-51628342.html.

55. Patagonia. Patagonia's Green Shipping Center. Available at http://www.patagonia.com/us/patagonia.go?assetid=2064, and for a video about the building see here http://www.youtube.com/watch?v=nr9WU4-NAc4.

56. Patagonia. 2011. 53 and growing – Announcing the opening of our latest Patagonia store. Available at http://www.thecleanestline.com/2011/01/53-and-growing-1.html.

57. Reinhardt, F. et al. 2011. Patagonia. Harvard Business School (9-711-020).

58. Hamm, S. 2006. A passion for the planet. *Bloomberg Businessweek Magazine*. Available at http://www.businessweek.com/stories/2006-08-20/a-passion-for-the-planet.

59. Malik, S. and Bidgoil, H. 2010. *The Handbook of Technology Management: Supply Chain Management, Marketing and Advertising, and Global Management Vol. 2* (Hoboken, NJ: John Wiley & Sons).

60. McKinnon, A. et al. 2010. *Green Logistics: Improving the Environmental Sustainability of Logistics* (London: Kogan Page Limited); Rodrigue, J. et al., 2013. *The Geography of Transport Systems* (New York: Green Logistics). Available at people.hofstra.edu/geotrans/eng/ch8en/appl8en/ch8a4en.html.

61. Pernecky, T. and Luck, M. 2012. *Events, Society and Sustainability: Critical and Contemporary Approaches* (Abingdon: Taylor & Francis).

62. Edahiro, J. 2011. A lesson from the March 11 quake and tsunami: An awareness of the importance of 'resilience'. *JFS Newsletter No. 112*. Available at http://www.japanfs.org/en/mailmagazine/newsletter/pages/031567.html.

63. American Independent Business Alliance. The multiplier effect of local independent businesses ownership. Available at www.amiba.net/resources/ multipliecr-effect; Institute for Local Self-Reliance. 2012. Community networks and economic development fact sheet. Available at http://www.ilsr.org/ content-types/fact-sheets-resource-archive/.

64. *Economics Online*. The multiplier effect. Available at http://www.economics online.co.uk/Managing_the_economy/The_multiplier_effect.html.

65. *Econbrowser*. Multiplier estimates, across countries, across states, across time. Available at http://www.econbrowser.com/archives/2011/07/multipliers_ acr.html.

66. King, D. et al. 1999. *Electronic Commerce: A Managerial Perspective* (Englewood Cliffs, NJ: Prentice Hall).

67. Zaiback, O. 2010. Customer service statistics for 2011. *Customer 1*. Available at http://www.customer1.com/blog/customer-service-statistics.

68. Watson, R. et al. 2012. The emergence of sustainability as the new dominant logic: Implications for information systems. Thirty-third International Conference on Information Systems, Orlando, FL.

69. Miller, K. 2010. Sustainability and the customer experience. *The Triple Pundit*. Available at http://www.triplepundit.com/2010/04/sustainability-customer-serviceand-the-customer-experience/.

70. Environmental Industry Associations: NSWMA & WASTEC. 2011. History of solid waste management, environmentalists everyday. Available at http://www. environmentalistseveryday.org/publications-solid-waste-industry-research/ information/history-of-solid-waste-management/index.php.

71. The Zero Waste Alliance. Welcome to the Zero Waste Alliance. Available at http://www.zerowaste.org/.

72. Meadows. D. et al. 2004. *Limits to Growth: The 30 Year Update* (White River Junction, VT: Chelsea Green Publishing Company).

130

73. *Merriam–Webster Online*. 2013. Technology, Def. 1(a).

74. Sankar, K and Bouchard, S., 2009. Enterprise Web 2.0 Fundamentals – Network World Chapter 9: Web 2.0 and Mobility. *Cisco Press*. Available at **www. networkworld.com/subnets/cisco/062609-ch9-web2-mobility.html**; Golden, F. 1999. Who built the first computer? *Time Magazine* (29 March). Available at **http://www.time.com/time/magazine/article/0,9171,990596,00.html**.

75. Daintith, J. and Wright, E. 2008. *A Dictionary of Computing* (Oxford: Oxford University Press).

76. Druker, P. The first technological revolution and its lessons. American Studies at the University of Virginia. Available at **http://xroads.virginia.edu/~DRBR/d_ rucker5.html**.

77. Hawken, P. 2007. *Blessed Unrest* (New York: Penguin Books).

78. Hilty, L. 2005. *Information Technology and Sustainability* (Hershey, PA: Idea Publishing Group); Hilty, L. 2011. Role of information technology to fight climate change stressed at UN meeting. *UN News Centre*. Available at **www.un.org/ apps/news/story.asp?NewsID=39031#.UUTX9FtARFx**.

79. Littlefield, M. and Roberts, M. 2012. Enterprise sustainability management: An emerging paradigm. *Environmental Leader*. Available at **www.environmental leader.com/2012/11/01/enterprise-sustainability-management-an-emerging-paradigm/**.

80. Musikanski, L. 2012. *How to Account for Sustainability* (Oxford: DōSustainability).

81. United States Green Building Council's LEED standards are available at **http:// new.usgbc.org/leed**.

82. Lesser, A., 2012. What eBay's bet on fuel cells means for the modern data center. *Gigaom*. Available at **http://gigaom.com/2012/10/30/what-ebays-bet-on-fl-cells-means-for-the-modern-data-center/**; Babcock, C., 2013. 5 data center trends for 2013. *Information Week*. Available at **www.informationweek.com/ hardware/data-centers/5-data-center-trends-for-2013/240145349**.

83. District Heating & Cooling. *Euro Heat & Power.* Available at http://www. euroheat.org/District-heating-cooling-4.aspx#What_is_District_Heating.

84. US Bank Locations, 2012. FSB financial information – One PacificCoast Bank. Available at http://www.usbanklocations.com/one-pacificcoast-bank-fsb-shore bank-pacific-branch-financial-info.html.

85. One PacificCoast Bank Beneficial Banking Report. Available at http://one pacificcoastbank.com/ContentPage.aspx?name=2012+Beneficial+Banking +Report.

86. One PacificCoast Vision. Available at http://onepacificcoastbank.com/ philosophy.aspx.

87. One PacificCoast 2012 Beneficial Banking Report. Available at http://one pacificcoastbank.com/ContentPage.aspx?name=2012+Beneficial+Banking +Report#Annual-Reportundefined&utm_source=Copy+of+Albina+Press+Rel ease+to+Community&utm_campaign=Albina+News+Desk+Press+Release& utm_medium=email.

88. Walker, A. 2012. One PacificCoast Bank joins the benefit corporation movement. *Reuters.* Available at http://www.reuters.com/article/2012/10/04/idUS10596 +04-Oct-2012+BW20121004.

89. B-Corp. Best for Overall Impact 50+ Employees. Available at http://best fortheworld.bcorporation.net/.

90. One PacificCoast Bank USA. Global Alliance for Banking on Values. Available at http://www.gabv.org/our-banks/onepacificcoast-bank.

91. One PacificCoast 2012 Beneficial Banking Report. Available at http://one pacificcoastbank.com/ContentPage.aspx?name=2012+Beneficial+Banking +Report#Annual-Reportundefined&utm_source=Copy+of+Albina+Press+Rel ease+to+Community&utm_campaign=Albina+News+Desk+Press+Release& utm_medium=email.

92. Green America. 2008. Responsible credit cards. Available at http://www.green america.org/livinggreen/ResponsibleCreditCards.cfm.

93. Member Profile: One PacificCoast Bank. Network of business innovation and sustainability. Available at http://nbis.org/one-pacific-coast-bank/.

94. HR Metrics Service. 2012. HR metrics & standards. Available at http://www.hrmetricsservice.org/0/pdf/standards_glossary.pdf.

95. USDA Headquarters Sustainable Operations. What is a green team? Available at http://greening.usda.gov/definition.htm.

96. Bureau of Planning and Sustainability – City of Portland. Green team guide: Sustainability at work. Available at http://sustainabilityatworkpdx.com/down loads/GreenTeamGuide_2012.pdf.

97. Herring, C. 2005. Does diversity pay?: Racial composition of firms and the business case for diversity. University of Illinois at Chicago and Institute of Government and Public Affairs University of Illinois (published online). Available at http://www.genderprinciples.org/resource_files/Does_Diversity_Pay-_Racial_Composition_of_Firms_and_The_Business_Case_for_Diversity.pdf.

98. Oxenburgh, M. et al. 2004. *Increasing Productivity and Profit through Health and Safety* (New York: Taylor & Francis, Inc.).

99. Kaplan, R. and Norton, D. 1996. Using the Balanced Scorecard as a strategic management system. *Harvard Business Review* (January–February): 71–79.

100. US Department of State Diplomacy in Action Ethics. Virtues and values: Knowing what matters most. Available at http://www.state.gov/m/a/os/64663.htm.

101. OECD/Statistical Office of the European Communities. *62005 Oslo Manual: Guidelines for Collecting and Interpreting Innovation Data*, 3rd edn (Luxembourg: OECD Publishing); and Grueber, M and Studt, T. 2012. Industrial R&D perspectives & forecasts. *R&D Mag.* Available at http://www.rdmag.com/articles/2012/12/industrial-r-d-perspectives-and-forecasts.

102. National Research Council. 2008. *Transitioning to Sustainability through Research and Development on Ecosystem Services and Biofuels: Workshop Summary* (Washington, DC: The National Academies Press).

103. Benyus, J. *A Biomimicry Primer, Biomimicry 3.8*. Available at http://biomimicry.
net/educating/professional-training/resource-handbook/.

For Product Safety Concerns and Information please contact our EU
representative GPSR@taylorandfrancis.com
Taylor & Francis Verlag GmbH, Kaufingerstraße 24, 80331 München, Germany

www.ingramcontent.com/pod-product-compliance
Ingram Content Group UK Ltd.
Pitfield, Milton Keynes, MK11 3LW, UK
UKHW040928180425
457613UK00011B/308